Selected Stories of the Western Frontier from "Indian Depredations in Texas" including Young, Jack, Palo Pinto, and Parker Counties

Selected Stories of the Western Frontier from "Indian Depredations in Texas" including Young, Jack, Palo Pinto, and Parker Counties

Indian depredations in Texas: reliable accounts of battles, wars, adventures, forays, murders, massacres, etc., etc., together with biographical sketches of many of the most noted Indian fighters and frontiersmen of Texas.

J.W. Wilbarger

Dedicated

TO THE MEMORY OF THE HEROIC FRONTIERSMEN
WHO BY THEIR SACRIFICES PREPARED THE WAY
FOR THE PROSPERITY WHICH TEXAS NOW ENJOYS,
I DEDICATE THIS BOOK.

The Author.

*Original Narratives of
Texas History and
Adventure*

Indian Depredations in Texas

By J. W. Wilbarger

A FACSIMILE REPRODUCTION OF THE ORIGINAL WITH SE-
LECTED TEXT FROM YOUNG, JACK, PALO PINTO, AND PARKER
COUNTIES

Inkwell Press

Figure : J.W. Wilbarger

Library of Congress Cataloging-in-Publication Data
Wilbarger, J. W. (John Wesley), 1806 - Indian depredations
in Texas: reliable accounts of battles, wars, adventures, forays, murders, massacres, etc., etc., together with biographical
sketches of many of the most noted Indian fighters and frontiersmen of Texas / by J.W. Wilbarger.
1. Indians of North America — Texas — Wars.
2. Indians of North America—Texas—History.
3. Frontier and pioneer life—Texas.
4. Texas — History. I. Title.

Library Cataloging Data
*Selected Stories of the Western Frontier in "Indian Depreda-
tions in Texas"* by J.W. Wilbarger
Library of Congress Control Number: 2026937215
ISBN: 979-8-89946-036-4 (Hardback), 979-8-89946-035-7 (Pa-
perback), 979-8-89946-034-0 (Kindle)
BISAC: HIS036050 HISTORY / United States / Civil War
Period (1850-1877)
BISAC: HIS036040 HISTORY / United States / 19th Century
BISAC: HIS036130 HISTORY/ United States / State & Local /
Southwest (AZ, NM, OK, TX)

Book Cover Design:
Created by Inkwell Press Staff.

Publisher Information
Inkwell Press, 2321 Sir Barton Way, Suite 140-1032, Lexington,
KY 40509
Web: https://inkwell.net
Published in the United States of America on acid-free paper

J.W. Wilbarger's original book, *Indian Depredations in Texas*, is extensive and documents numerous accounts of Indian attacks on settlers throughout the Western Frontier, from northern to southern Texas. For about twenty years Wilbarger gathered accounts of Indian attacks, incorporating approximately 250 separate encounters into the book. Numerous accounts were contributed by others who had personal, first-hand or second-hand knowledge of the events.

In the period of these Indian depredations (1820s–1870s), the western frontier was roughly along the 97th and 98th meridians.

According to my dictionary app, "Depredation" is defined as "the act of preying upon or plundering; robbery; ravage."

I have selected the stories from Young, Jack, Palo Pinto, and Parker counties for inclusion in this shorter book. I chose this group of counties given their importance in Texas's Western Frontier history, since they were the locations of key events—one of which ended Indian depredations across the frontier and effectively brought the Western Frontier to an end, opening the West to expansion without further contest.

First, note that the author's brother, Josiah Wilbarger, took part in what was likely among the first ghost stories documented in Texas. In the Preface to *Indian Depredations in Texas*, J.W. Wilbarger states:

"Josiah Wilbarger, who was scalped by the Indians a few miles east of where the capitol of Texas now is, was my brother. He survived, as this book relates, the massacre of his companions, but afterwards died from a disease of the skull caused by injuries."

This story is presented as the book's final chapter. The same episode is recounted by J. Frank Dobie in the chapter "The Dream That Saved Wilbarger" in his book *Tales of Old-Time Texas*. Dobie characterizes the tale of Josiah Wilbarger's scalping and the dream that saved his life as among Texas's best-known historical legends.

Between the 1850's and the mid-1870's, Indian raids made these four counties among the most dangerous areas in North America. Below is the author's articulation of this point in the chapter 'Murders in Palo Pinto County':

"WE do not hesitate in saying that there is no territory upon the face of the earth of equal dimensions to that embraced within the boundaries of Palo Pinto, Parker, Young and Jack counties, whose inhabitants have suffered as much at the hands of the blood thirsty savages as have those who, at an early day, peopled the counties above named."

This map from the University of Texas at Arlington shows the locations of "Interethnic" violent encounters of mostly Indians attacking settlers, and you can see that they are concentrated in these four counties (see the circle on the map below). The Western Frontier ran along these four counties until it ended.

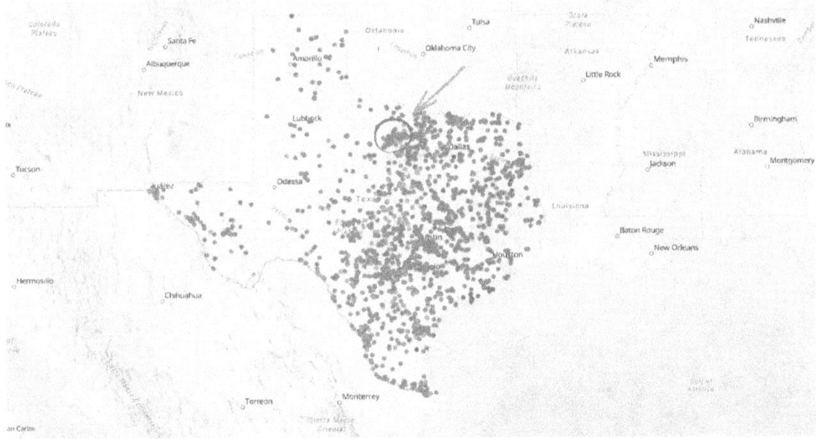

Figure : Map provided by the University of Texas in Arlington's "Texas in Turmoil: Mapping Interethnic Violence, 1821-1879" project. From UTA's website: "In 2015, the Center for Greater Southwestern Studies, working with the UTA Library's Digital Creation department, began work on a digital mapping project to better understand violence among the many peoples of Texas in the early decades of the nineteenth century. Titled "Border Land: Inter-ethnic Violence in 19th Century Texas," the website mapped sites of conflict from 1821 (Mexican independence) to statehood in 1846. In 2023 the Center and Library project team began work on Phase II of the project—now renamed Texas in Turmoil — to develop a site with more interactive features, enhanced search functions, and a data analytics component. Phase II also extended the timeframe of the project to 1879, to include Reconstruction and the end of the so-called "Indian Wars."

Each dot on this map denotes an "Interethnic violence" encounter. While the majority are Indian-on-Anglo-American attacks, the map also includes Anglo-American-on-Indian attacks; Indian-on-African American attacks (for example, the attack on Britt Johnson's family by the Kiowa and Comanche in the Elm Creek raid of 1864, and the attack on Britt Johnson and his African-American companions in 1871 by

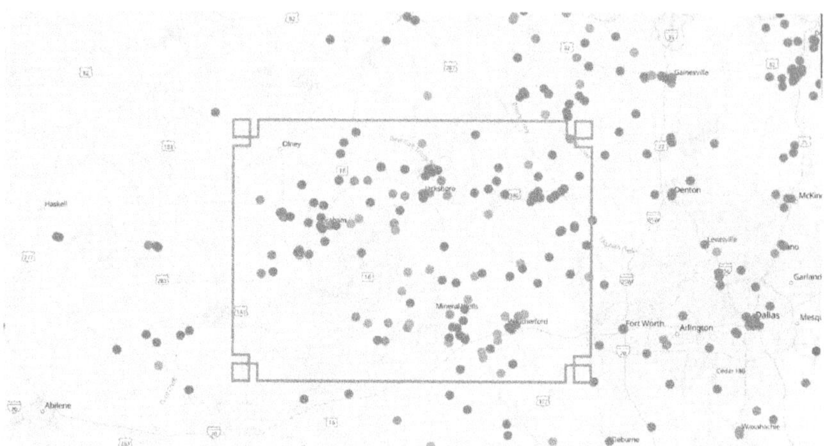

Figure : This is roughly the area involved in what is now Palo Pinto, Young, Jack, and Parker Counties. In this red square is also some of Wise county in the top right, but this square illustrates the activity in this area.

the Kiowa); Anglo-American-on-African American attacks; and other permutations of interethnic violence. These markers do not represent violence within ethnicities, so Indian-on-Indian attacks are omitted (in the history of the Western Frontier, Indian-on-Indian attacks and deaths outnumbered Indian-on-Anglo-American attacks and deaths).

The frontier, and particularly Northwest Texas, was a harsh and brutal environment: the nomadic Comanche and Kiowa relied on buffalo from the Great Plains and thus repeatedly collided with settlements that were expanding westward. Depicted in the circle is the quintessential Western Frontier, where tribes from the Great Plains engaged in raids aimed at achieving glory (for instance, elevating a warrior's standing by proving bravery), seizing horses, abducting captives, and carrying out retribution and terror. These four counties witnessed several consequential Western Frontier events: the Comanche gang rape and killing of Martha Sherman, led by Peta Nocona, which prompted the Battle of Pease River and the recovery of Cynthia Ann Parker; the Elm Creek Raid, which involved Britt Johnson's family; and the Warren Wagon Train Massacre and the ensuing trial of two Kiowa chiefs, an episode that established a new precedent in American legal jurisprudence, contributed to the Indian Wars, and helped bring about the end of the Western Frontier.

Martha Sherman, nine months pregnant, was attacked on the border of Parker and Palo Pinto counties. The day after the attack she gave birth to a stillborn infant. She died a few days later. She is buried at Willow Springs Cemetery in Weatherford. She was the great-great-grandmother of John R. Erickson, the author of the *Hank the Cowdog* books. He authored *Prairie Gothic: The Story of a West Texas Family*, which concerns Martha Sherman and his extended family.

In 1872, Fort Richardson in Jack County (in the city of Jacksboro) was the largest military fort in the United States and the most significant with respect to the U.S. Army's involvement in the Indian Wars.

Aggregating attacks across the four counties for the roughly twenty-year period during which the frontier existed here (mid 1850's–mid 1870's) produces a count of more than one hundred. In *History of Parker County and the Double Log Cabin*, G.A. Holland (mayor of Weatherford in the 1930's) states that Parker County experienced the most severe Indian raids. Holland wrote:

"It is estimated that from the first settlements in 1854 to the last raid in 1874, that within a radius of 100 miles—including Parker County, which was the worst sufferer—the Indians stole and destroyed six million dollars worth of property, killed and scalped or carried away about 400 hundred people into a captivity worse than death."

Adjusted for inflation, $6 million in 1874 corresponds to roughly $170 million in 2026. It is staggering that 400 people were kidnapped or killed from an area that was already sparsely populated.

In a letter of 1871 addressed to Washington, D.C., Weatherford's physician, I.P. Vollintine, wrote:

"Dear Sir,

As I live far off in the wilds of Texas you will be surprised to receive a letter from a stranger from these parts. I therefore write in behalf of our suffering frontier. Can there be nothing done for us? There have been no less than nine persons killed and scalped in the past three weeks in this vicinity, which can be verified by Genl. Oakes of Fort Richardson. We have applied to the military for assistance, and they have rendered all in their power, but are powerless. The Indians are kept at Fort Sill, some one hundred miles from here, and they come down and do their stealing and killing before the soldiers can come up. The pursuit is useless. We see our horses at Fort Sill that have not been stolen from us more than ten days, but it is impossible to get them. I would suggest to the government the only way to stop these Indians from depredating on us is to take their horses from them and suffer none to have any, and never let any leave the reservation without an escort, and those that will not come in and submit to the government to be considered hostile and so dealt with, then we will have peace. They have stolen millions of dollars worth of property in the last four or five years, and near one thousand persons murdered. The Indians that depredate on us are the Comanche, Kiowa, Cheyennes and Wacos. For God's sake see if anything can be done for us. Lay it before the government and ask all who sympathize with suffering humanity to come to our assistance. I have written quite a long letter, but hope you will give it a perusal at your leisure, and think of us in the far off West. Hoping to be excused for this long letter, I remain your most obedient servant."

I.P. Vollintine

Dr. Vollintine was missing his right hand at the wrist. His grave is located at City Greenwood Cemetery in Weatherford, TX. It was perhaps this letter, and certainly other letters like it, that compelled President Ulysses S. Grant to send General William Tecumseh Sherman to these counties in 1871 and make a tour of the Western Frontier and see for himself if what these letters said was true about the settler's dire situation regarding Indian attacks, kidnappings, etc., on the frontier.

General Sherman traveled from San Antonio to points north and west, visiting forts established as defensive positions to protect settlements from raiding Native American groups. The forts, however, were so widely dispersed and so sparsely manned that they were ineffective at protecting settlements that were continuing to encroach westward onto the Great Plains.

Upon his arrival at Fort Griffin, General Sherman met with local residents who described the realities of frontier life. Among those he met were Elizabeth Ann Clifton, Isaiah Clifton, and Charlotte Durkin (Elizabeth Ann's granddaughter). During the Elm Creek Raid, Elizabeth and Charlotte were taken captive; the Kiowa and Comanche also captured Britt Johnson's wife and his two remaining children, having killed his eldest son during the attack. Riding alone on horseback into Indian territory, Britt Johnson succeeded in ransoming his family and consequently became regarded as a frontier hero. He was, however, killed in January 1871 by the Kiowa in Young County while hauling supplies along Salt Creek Prairie to Fort Griffin.

It is an irony of history that the same Kiowa chief, Maman-ti — described as a very sinister medicine man and the leader of the raid that killed Britt Johnson only months earlier — now commanded a raiding party of approximately 150 warriors who watched General Sherman from behind a hill as his party crossed Salt Creek Prairie, traveling east from Fort Belknap to Fort Richardson in May, 1871.

General Sherman escaped the fate of Britt Johnson — who was buried a short distance from the hill where the Kiowa were hiding — because Maman-ti, called the "Owl Prophet" since his medicine allowed him to commune with owls, had communed with an owl the night before. According to the book *The Indian Trial* by Charles M. Robinson III, here's how it happened:

"In the Kiowa camp, Maman-ti was making medicine. He sat apart from the others, who were grouped together in silence waiting for some message to the do-ha-te from a dead ancestor. Soon they heard the cry of an owl and the soft beat of his wings. The Do-ha-te stood, raised his arms and repeated what the owl had told him.

"Two parties of Tehennas will pass...The first will be a small party. Perhaps we could overcome it easily. Many of you will be eager to do so. But it must not be attacked. The medicine forbids. Later... another party will come. This one may be attacked. The attack will be successful."

In short, General Sherman's life was spared because Maman-ti received a message from an owl. General Sherman, the highest-ranking officer in the United States Army and in full command of it, was largely responsible for the Union Army's victory in the Civil War, and had become famous (infamous) for his "march to the sea" in Georgia, lighting the Confederacy's cities and infrastructure ablaze. Nevertheless, on the Western Frontier in Young County, he was vulnerable and at the mercy of 150 Kiowa and Comanche who were watching him in silence. General Sherman, accompanied by General Randolph B. Marcy and by 17 men of the tenth infantry—all African Americans (buffalo soldiers)—passed the hill where the Kiowa were concealed. General Sherman and his men were outnumbered ten to one, and some Kiowa possessed repeating rifles. General Sherman and his fellow travelers were entirely unaware of the Kiowa as they ambled along Salt Creek Prairie.

The second party was a team of twelve men with ten wagons, transporting supplies westward from Weatherford to Fort Griffin. These men were employed by Weatherford businessman Henry Warren, although Warren was not present with the wagon train. The attack on these twelve men took place at Salt Creek Prairie, just where General Sherman had passed earlier.

I have been to Salt Creek Prairie, climbed the hill where the Kiowa were concealed, and stood at the location of the attack. I can hardly imagine what it would have been like to see 150 Kiowa and Comanche warriors descending that hill, running or riding horses at full speed, with Kiowa women trilling their tongues and the sound of war cries from the men as they rushed forward for battle.

Salt Creek Prairie has been described in historical accounts as the deadliest prairie in Texas. It may be argued that it was the deadliest place in North America at the time. Earlier, in April of 1871, while Ranald Mackenzie traversed the same route from Fort Griffin to Fort Richardson that General Sherman now followed in May, Mackenzie's captain, Robert G. Carter, recorded twenty-one graves along Salt Creek Prairie.

The Kiowa and Comanche swarmed and immediately killed three of the wagon train; seven men attempted to escape on foot by running east toward the trees on Cox Mountain. Two of them were killed while attempting to flee. Sam Elliot, wounded in the initial barrage, hid inside a wagon. Following the initial attack, the Indians stepped away from the wagons to search for signs of life and to determine whether there were any survivors who might still threaten them. Hau-tau, an eager young Kiowa on his first raid, ran forward and placed his hand on the wagon where Sam Elliot was hiding, and declared, "I claim the wagon and all that is in it!" In that instant, Sam Elliot pulled back the canvas and shot Hau-tau in the face. In shock and fury, the Kiowa ripped through the wagons. When they got ahold of Sam Elliot, they cut his tongue out and roasted him to death over a fire.

While running towards Cox mountain, Thomas Brazeal suffered dual wounds to the same foot—one inflicted by an arrow and the other by a bullet. At some point on the 20-mile route to Fort Richardson, his companions carried him to a ranch, mounted horses there, and rode to Fort Richardson. Arriving in the middle of the night, they roused everyone and reported the raid, notifying General Sherman and Ranald Mackenzie.

At that moment the event became vividly personal for Sherman: he realized that it might have been him shot full of bullet holes and arrows and lying dead and bloated on the prairie, since he had passed that very spot the day before the wagon train was attacked. Sherman immediately dispatched Ranald Mackenzie to assess the scene and track down the Indians if possible. Robert Carter, who was riding with Mackenzie, wrote what they encountered at the site in his book *On the Border with Mackenzie, or Winning West Texas from the Comanches*:

> "There could be nothing more appalling, heart rending or sickening to the human senses than the spectacle which was witnessed when our command reached the scene of the Salt Creek Prairie massacre. The poor victims were stripped, scalped, and horribly mutilated; several were beheaded and their brains scooped out. Their fingers, toes and private parts had been cut off

and stuck in their mouths, and their bodies, now lying in several inches of water and swollen or bloated beyond all chance of recognition, were filled full of arrows which made them resemble porcupines. Their bowels had been gashed with knives and carefully heaped upon each exposed abdomen had been placed a mass of live coals, now of course, extinguished by the deluge of water which was still coming down with a torrential power almost indescribable.

Our retched man, Samuel Elliot, who, fighting hard to the last, had evidently been wounded, was founded chained between two wagon wheels and, a fire having been made from the wagon pole, he had been slowly roasted to death — "burnt to a crisp." That he was still alive when the fiendish torture was begun, was shown by his limbs being drawn up and contracted."

In total, seven members of the wagon train were killed. Hau-tau lived until he was brought back to Fort Sill, and subsequently died when screwworms reached his brain. Altogether, three Kiowa were killed.

Wilbarger recounts the Warren Wagon Train Massacre in this book; for a more thorough account of the event and the subsequent capital murder trials of two Kiowa chiefs who were among the attack's leaders, read *The Indian Trial* by Charles M. Robinson III.

The monument and the hill from which the Kiowa hid are both on private property. As a point of clarification, Satanta, Satank, and Big Tree were all Kiowa chiefs. The employer of

Figure : The Warren Wagon Train Massacre monument, which reads "Buried here are the remains of seven teamsters, Nathan S. Long, N.J. Baxter, Jesse Bowman, James S. and Samuel E. Elliott, James and Thomas Williams, employed by Henry Warren, government contractor, who were slain by Indians under Satanta, Satank, and Big Tree, Kiowa and Comanche Chiefs, on May 18, 1871 while hauling forage between Jacksboro and Fort Griffin".

the men and owner of the wagons, Henry Warren, had erected a wooden monument in this spot, that was mentioned by M.K. Kellogg in his book *Texas Journal* (1872), that read "Sacred to the memory of seven brave men killed by Indians at this place on Thursday, May 18, 1871, while in discharge of their duty defending their train against 150 Comanche Indians. N.S. Song - Wagon Master, Teamsters: J.S. Elliott, Sam Elliott, N.J. Baxter, Jas. Williams, John Mullins, Jesse Bowman." There are a few discrepancies between these two monuments. To clear them up, let me say that it was mostly Kiowa who participated in the attack (with only some Comanche included), the three chiefs were Kiowa, Nathan S. Long is likely the correct name of the wagon master (not Song), and Thomas Williams' name was likely incorrectly added on the state's monument, and likely Henry Warren's monument was correct which listed John Mullins as among the men who were killed.

The trials of the Kiowa chiefs (Satanta and Big Tree were tried separately) were sensational; news outlets from across the United States filled the Jacksboro courthouse. This marked the first occasion in American history on which Indians were tried in a criminal court. S.W.T. Lanham, the prosecuting attorney, attained fame as a result of the trial and subsequently served as governor of Texas. Both Lanham and the defense attorney, Joe Woolfolk, resided in the same neighborhood in Weatherford; their houses still stand. Henry Warren held part ownership of a building later sold to S.W.T. Lanham, which Lanham used as his law office. The building remains in use on Weatherford's downtown square. To the best of my knowledge, this is the oldest building in downtown Weatherford — it is known as the Franco–Texas Land Company building.

When questioned at Fort Sill by the Indian Agent about the wagon train attack, Satanta told the Indian Agent that it was he and other chiefs who were responsible for the attack. General Sherman arrested Satanta, Satank, and Big Tree and told the rest of the Kiowa to return the 41 mules that had been stolen from the wagon train.

Only two of the Kiowa chiefs (Satanta and Big Tree) were tried in a court of law; the third chief that was arrested, Satank, never reached trial. Shortly after the party left Fort Sill for Jacksboro, he cut or chewed sufficient flesh from his wrists to free himself from the handcuffs, took a soldier's carbine rifle and knocked the soldier out of the wagon. While trying to use the gun, he was shot and killed by the other soldiers who were transporting them. They left him by the roadside; after some time had passed and no Kiowa came to retrieve him, soldiers from Fort Sill returned his body to Fort Sill, where he was buried. Satank was in his 70's, and was the leader of the 10-man elite fighting force within the Kiowa that were called the koitsenko (the Special Forces equivalent of Kiowa warriors).

Following the Warren Wagon Train Massacre, General Sherman directed the United States Army to undertake offensive campaigns and to consign the remaining Indian strongholds to reservations; he dispatched Ranald Mackenzie into unfamiliar Indian territory to confront Quanah Parker and the Quahadi Comanches in west Texas (including Palo Duro Canyon), pursued the Kickapoo, Lipan Apache, and Mescalero Apache in Mexico who had raided south Texas, engaged the Ute in Colorado, and defeated the Lakota Sioux and Cheyenne, the tribes that had massacred General Custer. These and other U.S. Army campaigns against Native American tribes are collectively termed the Indian Wars.

24

Figure : Satanta (White Bear), Kiowa Chief

Figure : Big Tree, Kiowa Chief. Credit: DeGolyer Library, Southern Methodist University

Ranald Mackenzie's definition of success was to keep as many people alive as possible on both sides, but to destroy the means and infrastructure of the Indians by burning their teepees and cooking utensils etc., and killing their horses, thereby removing their means of fighting, in which case they had no choice but to go onto the reservations. Destroying thee enemy's infrastructure was exactly what Sherman and

Mackenzie had done to the Confederacy to help win the Civil War.

After the relocation of the remaining Indians onto reservations, the government arrested in excess of 70 people from several tribes and transported them to St. Augustine, Florida. Subsequent to the Indian Wars and the arrests and exile to Florida, raids on the settlements ceased. Consequently, the Warren Wagon Train Massacre triggered a sequence of events which ultimately brought about the end of the Western Frontier.

Several of the stories above (and others) appear in what could be described as the finest literature written about any part of Texas, *Goodbye to a River* by John Graves. Mr. Graves's river was the Brazos, which flows through these four counties. He embarked on a three-week canoe journey along the Brazos in 1957, commencing at Possum Kingdom Lake, passing through what is now Lake Granbury, and finishing shortly above Lake Whitney. He narrated the frequently violent and fatal encounters between Indians and settlers.

Only minor spelling mistakes in J.W. Wilbarger's text have been corrected in this book, and a newly created index accompanies this book. The chapter Indian Warfare on the Northwestern Border is included because it relates stories that occurred in this area.

My sincere gratitude to my wife, Whitney Akins, and to our children for allowing me the time necessary to complete this work. I am especially grateful to Bill Dembski and Chloe Dembski of Inkwell Press for granting me the freedom to publish Western Frontier history and for the friendship extended by the Dembski family. I also thank my mother, Fran Smith; my brother, Bill Akins; my father-in-law Kelly Beard; and my friends Mike Gilliam, Anthony Aquino, Victor Sauceda, Brandon Hughes, Tom Moudy, Brandon Broyles and Michael Lum for their encouragement in these studies and for patiently listening as I regale them with Western Frontier history. Tom and I visited the site of the Warren Wagon Train Massacre together. Those interested in this history should visit the Young County Museum of History and Culture. And special thanks to Shannon Potts.

Table of Contents

Chapter 1

Murders in Palo Pinto County

1858

WE do not hesitate in saying that there is no territory upon the face of the earth of equal dimensions to that embraced within the boundaries of Palo Pinto, Parker, Young and Jack counties, whose inhabitants have suffered as much at the hands of the blood thirsty savages as have those who, at an early day, peopled the counties above named. From 1858 up to 1875, Indian raids were frequent, and they scarcely ever visited the settlements without carrying with them a large number of horses, and generally a few scalps of the settlers ornamented their belts as they passed out of the settlements to their homes in the mountains or on the staked plains, and not unfrequently these trophies were carried with them to the reservation, where the Indians were being cared for by the United States government. The list of murders which we here present, simply represents a very few of the many outrages committed by the Indians in that section of the country. It may not unfrequently happen that errors will be detected in the following narratives, but this was almost unavoidable, for at the time the data was obtained (some fifteen years prior to going to press) from which these articles were written, there were no railroads in that section of the State and settlers were rather scarce. We have been unable since then to have corrections made in every instance, but trust there will be no serious errors found in any of them. It has been almost impossible to get the correct dates in every instance, but in most cases they will be found correct, as reliable frontiersmen have been found who kept a diary in which the dates of most of the murders have been recorded. The first murder of which we have any account in Palo Pinto county is that of John Edwards, a lad about seven years of age. Young Edwards was playing in the lot when five Indians suddenly rushed upon him, tore his scalp from his head then turned him loose. They took so large a scalp from the boy's head that the skin fell down over his eyes, blinding him, and he was compelled to raise it with one hand to enable him to see. The Indians then started to the house of the boy's parents, but Mrs. Edwards saw them approaching and barred the doors. Fortunately for her at this moment Mr. Edwards and his herders came up, driving some cattle, and as soon as the Indians heard them they fled. The little boy who was scalped lived several months afterwards, but finally died from the effects of the wound.

The next victims of whom we have any account were Benjamin F. Baker, William M. Peters and Henry Welty. These men were all killed by the Indians in 1863. During the winter of 1863 a party of Indians came down the Brazos river on the east side into Parker county. They stole a large number of horses, and to avoid pursuit they crossed to the west side of the river and went out through Palo Pinto county.

They had gone but a short distance on the west side when they came across Mr. Baker, who was traveling alone. The Indians waylaid him and shot him from the brush. This was on Saturday, February 28, 1863. Baker had left his home in the morning and had gone over to a neighbor's, Doctor G. P. Barber, for some pork. After getting the pork he started back home and had gotten about one-fourth of a mile from Barber's house when he was attacked by eight or ten Indians. They ran him back to Barber's, and in the chase shot four arrows into him, two in his back, one in his arm and one in his thigh. He remained on his horse, however, until he arrived at Barber's fence gate, where he fell off his horse, dead. Barber hearing the noise ran out with his gun, which he presented at the Indians and prevented them from scalping him. They did not molest the house but got the horse Baker was riding and then went to Barber's lot and took his horse out and then departed. J. H. Baker, a nephew of Benjamin F. Baker, who then, as now, lived in Palo Pinto county, was the nearest neighbor of Doctor Barber and had seen his uncle pass his house during the morning while on his way to Barber's. The sudden death of his uncle was, of course, a great shock to the nephew (who was notified of the fact during the afternoon) and it devolved upon the latter to communicate this sad intelligence to the family of the deceased. The scene at the household was one never to be forgotten by the kinsman who bore the sad tidings. The following day the remains of Mr. Baker were carried to town for burial by the nephew, who first carried them by the home of the deceased, that his wife and children might take their last look upon the cold, pale face of the husband and father. The death of Mr. Baker cast a gloom over the entire community. He was among the earliest settlers of Palo Pinto county, having come to Texas and settled in the county in 1857, and had passed through many privations and hardships, such as are incident to a frontier life. He was a native of Ashe county, North Carolina.

We will now follow up the Indians after leaving Barber's house. At what point we do not know, but it was during the same day of the killing of Baker that this party of Indians came upon William M. Peters. Mr. Peters also moved into Palo Pinto county in about the year 1857, afterwards married there, and at the time of his death was living about thirteen miles south of the town of Palo Pinto.

On the day mentioned he had occasion to go to the town of Palo Pinto, and from there he intended to go to the residence of his father. The morning he left he seemed uneasy and unwilling to start. He kissed his baby, and before leaving he kissed his wife and told her good bye, as he was going on a long journey. The horse he intended riding was a very poor one, and his wife advised him to ride another; but he replied, no, that it would take too much time to get another one. Whilst on his way, and just as he was entering a large prairie, he was attacked by a party of mounted Indians. His horse being exceedingly slow, there was no chance of escape. The Indians pressed him closely, and finally he dismounted and ran into an old deserted ranch house. As he entered the door many bullets struck the door facing above and on each side. Here he seems to have made a desperate fight and to have kept the Indians at bay for some time, as many bullets were found lodged in the walls, which had been fired at him by the Indians. Finally a ball struck him in the forehead and killed him. The Indians took his scalp and left.

During the fall of the same year Henry Welty met with a fate similar to that of Baker and Peters. He was born in Arkansas in 1818. He immigrated to Texas at an early day and lived for many years in Falls county. In 1846, he moved up the Brazos river into Palo Pinto county, where he followed the occupation of farming and stock raising without being molested to any great extent by the Indians. About the tenth of November, 1863, Welty took his gun and went out on foot in search of some stock. When he had gone about a half or three-quarters of a mile from his residence he was attacked by a party of Indians who had concealed themselves in a clump of shin oak bushes. After shooting him with a gun and several arrows, they cut his throat, scalped him, stripped him of his clothes and slashed the flesh from his limbs with their butcher knives. His body lay in this condition for three days before it was found by some of his neighbors. He was a brave and true man, and loved by all who knew him. He left a wife and three children to mourn his loss

Marcus L. Dalton was one of the earliest settlers of Palo Pinto county, and like most of those who cast their lots in that section of the country engaged in the stock business. By close attention to business and shrewd trading he soon accumulated a considerable stock around him, and made frequent drives to the territories. It was while he was returning home from one of these successful drives, that he met with his tragic death. Dalton was returning home from Kansas, at which place he had disposed of a la͡rge herd of cattle and had with him the proceeds of the sale, when he was attacked and killed by the Indians. On his return to Texas, he was accompanied by James Redfield and James McCaster. On the morning of the sixteenth of December, 1870, these three men left the residence of Dr. J. P. Volentine (brother-in-law of Dalton), in Weatherford, for Dalton's home on the Brazos. They had reached about the northeast corner of Palo Pinto county, when they were attacked by a party of Indians. The three men were riding in a buggy or ambulance and, of course, had no chance to escape from the Indians who were on horseback. The Indians soon killed all three of the men —then scalped and butchered them in a horrible manner. They also carried off several head of horses and a pair of mules. Before leaving they broke open the trunk, took out the clothing, and such articles as they did not care for, were scattered around over the ground. They failed to find, however, eleven thousand four hundred dollars, which Dalton had concealed in an old shoe which lay inside the trunk. Mr. Dalton left quite a large family, and many of them reside in Palo Pinto county. His widow, Mrs. Lucinda Dalton, and three of his sons, to wit: Charles A., George W. and Robert S. Dalton, all reside at this time —1888, in Palo Pinto county. His two sons, W. C. and G. L. Dalton, and his daughter, Mrs. Jane Volentine (wife of Dr. J. P. Volentine), are residents of Weatherford. Parker county. His eldest son, John Dalton, lives in the Pan Handle, of Texas, and one of his daughters, Mrs. Mary Hoover, wife of Frank Hoover, lives in Young county, Texas. Prior to the attack upon Dalton and his companions, but on the same day, George and Richard Joel had a fight with the same party of Indians, and forced them to retreat. It was during this retreat that they came up with Dalton's party. On the following day the bodies of the three men were discovered by Green Lassiter, while passing through Loving's Valley, and recognizing the body of Dalton, had the remains of the three men interred, and then carried the news to Weatherford. Poor fellow! little did he dream then that a similar fate awaited him only a few months later, but alas! too true. It was during the fall of the following year, we believe, that a party of Indians came down from the Wichita mountains, and began pillaging and plundering in their usual way. It was not long before they had collected a large number of horses, but before getting out of the country were discovered by some one on the range, who gave the settlers the alarm, and a party was quickly raised and in pursuit. The Indians were soon overtaken—a fight ensued—and Lassiter, who was one of the pursuing party was killed.

Chesley S. Dobbs and Jesse B. Veale were both residents of Palo Pinto county. The first named was killed in the year 1872, and the other in the following year. On June 26, 1872, Dobbs left his home and went to the town of Palo Pinto to buy some goods for his family. He reached the town in safety, made his purchases, and left for home—but the poor fellow was fated never to see it again. Failing to reach home at the appointed time, his wife became uneasy, and sent one of her sons in search of him. He went to the town of Palo Pinto, and learned that his father had been there, made his purchases, and gone home. The son of Dobbs was satisfied that some accident had happened to the old man, and raised a small party of men to aid him in searching for his father. They found the old man about half way between his house and town, killed, scalped and stripped of his clothes. The next day his clothes and scalp were recovered by a party of men who pursued the Indians. The Indians were taken by surprise and several of them killed. Clinton Dobbs, who now lives in Shackleford county, is a son of Chesley S. Dobbs.

Mr. Veale, we believe, was a native of Texas. On the twenty-fifth day of February, 1873, he. in company with some others, went on a fishing excursion into Palo Pinto county. After fishing a while, some of the party, Veale among the number, went into the woods in search of game, and accidentally came across some Indian horses that were hoppled. They took the horses and drove them to their fishing camp. One of the parties while driving the horses lost his powder horn, and Veale and J. E. Corbin went back to hunt for it. In the meantime the Indians had returned to the place where they had left their horses hoppled, and finding them gone, they determined to have revenge. They discovered Veale and his companion coming back, secreted themselves, and awaited their approach. As soon as they were within close range, the Indians fired on them, and Veale was so badly wounded he was unable to escape. His companion, being unhurt, made good his retreat. The Indians pressed him closely, but he had a repeating rifle which he fired several times at them with such deadly effect that they finally abandoned the chase, and went back to where they had shot Veale, carrying with them their wounded. They took refuge in a cave near by, and the Texans endeavored to drive them from it, but after several men had been wounded, they found it was impossible to dislodge them. The Texans then went to where Veale had been shot, and found him sitting at the root of a tree, dead. Before he died, however, he succeeded in sending one of the Indians to his "happy hunting ground". The Texans committed a great error in taking the Indian horses. They should have concealed themselves in the vicinity, and when the Indians came for them they could probably have killed them all with but little risk to themselves. Veale was killed at the mouth of Ioni Creek, on the Brazos. His mother and two of his brothers still reside in the town of Palo Pinto. He was a Mason, and was buried with Masonic honors on Wednesday, February 26, 1873.

Chapter 2

Massacres in Parker County

1859

THE name of Parker seems to be an ill-fated one in Texas when taken in connection with the Indian history of our country. Parker county was named for the venerable Isaac Parker, who, in the year 1855, represented that county (which then embraced a much larger territory than now) in the Legislature. He belonged to the Parker family who came to Texas in 1833, and settled in Montgomery county, now Grimes county. This same family of Parkers, with a few others, settled in Limestone county a little later, and in the year 1835 built Parker's fort, of historic fame, near where the town of Groesbeck now stands. The full history of the "Parker Fort Massacre " appears elsewhere in this volume. It will be seen from the long list of murders at the hands of the Indians as having occurred in Parker county and herein recorded, which list is but a very partial one, that no other county in the State furnishes a history with such a bloody record of barbaric cruelty.

Among the first murders which took place in Parker county and which in after years was never surpassed in savage duplicity and barbaric cruelty was that of Mrs. Sherman. During the year 1859 there lived two families, John Brown and ------- Sherman, in the northwestern portion of Parker county, on Rock creek, near the line of Palo Pinto, some three or four miles apart. This was from twelve to fifteen miles from the town of Weatherford, the county seat of Parker county. In the month of December, 1859, a party of marauding Indians made a raid into Parker and adjoining counties, stealing horses and committing murders wherever they went. Their presence was first made known in Parker county when they attacked John Brown, who was on the range, about one-half mile from his house, looking after his horses. He was surrounded by a party of five or six Indians, shot and speared to death and then scalped. The Indians carried off several head of horses. They then proceeded to his residence, but Mrs. Brown seeing them coming barred the doors and thereby saved herself, as the Indians were afraid to attack it, thinking probably there were men inside to defend it. From there they proceeded to Mr. Thompson's farm, at which place they increased their number of stolen horses to some twenty-five or thirty head. The marauding party had divided up into squads and before arriving at the residence of Mr. Sherman they had collected together and now numbered about fifty-six. When the Indians approached the house the family, consisting of six persons, were at dinner (one account we have says they were at breakfast, this, however, is immaterial). Several Indians galloped up to the yard fence, alighted from their horses, went into the house and cordially shook hands with the family, making the most friendly demonstrations. After this exhibition of savage duplicity these devils incarnate told the family to "vamose, vamose, Indians no hurt." The presence of so many Indians, of course, very much alarmed the family, but owing to the disadvantage at which they were placed, both by the sudden appearance and the superior number of the Indians, resistance was not to be thought of. Nothing was left for the family but to do as they were directed.

It was a cold rainy day, but the unfortunate family not wishing to incur the displeasure of these savages, started off upon their journey through the forests. They had only gone about half a mile, however, when a party of the fiendish band overtook them and ordered Mrs. Sherman to return to the house. The bereaved husband and children implored them not to take away the one they loved so dearly, but their entreaties were of no avail. The Indians said "they wanted squaw," and without further ceremony tore the unfortunate woman from the embrace of those she loved so dearly. She was taken back to the house and subjected to all manner of torture, barbaric cruelty, and brutal treatment too horrible to relate. Let the imagination picture if it can, this terrible tragedy—a description of it will not be attempted here.

The agonizing screams of the victim seemed to delight the heartless monsters, and it was not until they had inflicted upon this poor woman every character of punishment which their devilish minds could invent, that they could make up their minds to leave. Not satisfied to leave Mrs. Sherman to survive, if she could, the trying ordeal through which she had passed, they deliberately stripped her of all her clothing, shot several arrows into her body, and when ready to leave, two Indians on horseback rode up on either side and each taking hold of her, dashed off, while a third Indian followed behind and beat her in the back with a heavy stick. Finally, she fell almost lifeless upon the ground, when an Indian warrior dismounted, passed his knife around her head, and tore off her scalp. She was then left for dead, but after the Indians had departed, she revived sufficiently to crawl to the house, where she was soon found by her husband, who in the meantime had taken his children to a neighbor's, and had gotten a few friends to return with him to look after his wife. She was found in the condition we have just described, suffering a thousand deaths from wounds received, and indignities to which she had been subjected.

When she beheld her husband upon his return, by an effort almost superhuman, she rallied sufficiently to relate to her bereaved companion the sad story of all her sufferings at the hands of these merciless demons. Mrs. Sherman lived four days after this cruel treatment. The day following the perpetration of this outrage, the children were taken back home to take a last look at their dying mother. The meeting was one never to be forgotten by those who witnessed the tragic and heartrending scene. We would be glad that the catalogue of murders might end here, but this is but the beginning in that section.

Chapter 3

General Baylor's Fight on Paint Creek

1860

THE Browning boys were native Texans, and lived with their father on the Clear Fork of the Brazos river, and we think, in Stephens county. But the surrounding circumstances, and the fight of General Baylor with the Indians immediately after their attack upon the Browning boys, all tend to make this a proper place to record this incident among the list of Parker county massacres. During the month of June, 1860, a large party of Indians came down the Clear Fork of the Brazos on one of their raids. After committing numerous depredations they came upon Josephus and Frank Browing, who were out on the range hunting stock. It seems they had gotten down off their horses for the purpose of letting them graze. The horse of Josephus was hoppled. Upon the approach of the Indians the boys made for their horses, hoping to escape by flight, as they had no arms with which to make a defense. The Indians were pressing them so closely that Josephus saw he would surely be overtaken if he waited to unhopple his horse, so he mounted him as he was, and started with his brother. The Indians, of course, soon came up with him, and quickly dispatched him. Frank being on an unhoppled horse, made better speed, but the Indians were well mounted, closed in on him and wounded him in several places. Finally he reached Hubbard's creek, which was swimming and plunged into it just in time to escape the foremost Indians, who were rapidly gaining on him. The Indians seeing that they would have to swim the creek if they followed him further, gave up the chase and left.

The news of this sad affair soon reached the ears of General John R. Baylor, who happened to be in that section of the country, with a small party on a cow hunt. We take the following account of the fight, which ensued from H. Smythe's *Historical Sketch of Parker county*:

"In June of 1860, General John R. Baylor, who now resides in San Antonio, with his brother, George W. Baylor, his two sons, Walker K. and John W. Baylor, and Wat Reynolds, visited the Clear Fork of the Brazos, where the General formerly lived. While there hunting cattle, these gentlemen were informed of the killing of Josephus Browning, and the serious wounding of Frank Browning, by a large body of Comanches. They immediately went to the Browning ranch, on the Clear Fork, near the mouth of Hubbard's creek, where they met other gentlemen who had been attracted to the spot by the murderous acts of the Indians. General Baylor, George W. Baylor, Elias Hale, Minn Wright and John Dawson started in pursuit of the demons, and on the fifth day, June 28, overtook them on Paint creek, where a fierce contest ensued, during which Baylor and his friends killed thirteen of the Indians. On their return to Weatherford they brought the scalps of nine of them, together with numerous trophies, including the scalp of a white woman whom the Indians had killed, several bows and arrows, darts, quivers, shields, tomahawks and other paraphernalia of savage warfare. The feeling against the Indians was so bitter that Baylor and his party were decidedly lionized for their prowess and daring. The horrible murder of Mrs. Sherman and others in the northwestern portion of the county, in 1859, and other similar outrages, were fresh in the minds of the people, who seemingly delighted in the slaughter of any of the hostile bands. The excitement was very great. The news of Baylor's success extended to the adjoining counties, and the heroic men were honored by a public barbecue on the square, which was participated in by several hundred people. Speeches were made and general rejoicings were universal. In the evening of the day a dance was indulged in at the court house, which was kept up "until broad day light," the following morning. In the long room a rope was stretched diagonally across, and on it were hung the nine Indian scalps, the woman's scalp captured from the defunct Comanches, and all the trophies of the expedition. In the excitement incident to the glorification, those who participated in the festivities evidently forgot that the prominent decorations of the hall were the unmistakable evidences of death and murder, and the relics of a barbarism then very frequent in this section of Texas.

General Baylor took his scalps and other spoils of the victors to various cities and towns, and soon after the people of the southeastern portion of the State sent flour, meal and all kinds of provisions, clothing, boots and shoes, blankets, pistols, guns, etc., to Weatherford for the support and protection of the people of the frontier. These supplies came in large quantities and served a most excellent purpose.

There was one universal cry. It seemed to be the heartfelt desire of every person. "Exterminate the Indians," was the watchword, and it is not to be wondered that such was the case, when we fully realize the vast destruction of property and human life. Up to the close of 1875 it is estimated that the Indians captured and destroyed property, within a circle of one hundred miles of Parker county, worth at least six millions of dollars, and killed and took into captivity nearly four hundred persons! The reservations, nine miles below Belknap, and twelve miles above, in Young county, on which were upwards of one thousand Indians, were broken up and the savages driven beyond the Red river on the north and the Pease river on the west. Colonel Robert S. Neighbors was the government Indian agent and Shapley Ross of Waco the reservation agent. Yet, with all the terror and devastation of those days and the insecurity of persons and property in this very section of Texas then, no portion of the great States of New York, Pennsylvania or Ohio can boast of more security than the Texas frontier—even one hundred and fifty miles beyond Parker county—enjoys today. The periodic predatory incursions of these wild men are ended. Civilization and population have driven them far away from any possible danger from them and rendered our county and vicinity places of very decided safety."

[Note.—The book from which this was taken was published in 1877.]

It may not be inappropriate to here narrate an incident that took place possibly the latter part of the same year, or the first of the next. Baylor gave notice to the young men that he was going to take a grand buffalo hunt and wanted the boys to take a hand in it. As this announcement was made about the beginning of the war, a good many thought that Baylor's object was to capture the United States posts along the frontier, but be this as it may, he raised a considerable force with which he proceeded far out on the plains, and although they took no government posts they did have a glorious time in hunting and killing buffalo. When they were tired of the sport they turned their faces towards the settlements and reached Camp Cooper in safety. The Colonel and his men, thinking they were beyond all danger, be took themselves to rest without placing any guards on post, forgetting, it seems, that it was a common practice with the Indians to follow parties returning to the settlements with out making any attack upon them until they thought themselves safe from all danger. The Indians were shrewd enough to know that when in or near the settlements they would not naturally be as watchful as when they were within the enemy's country.

Early one morning while the Colonel and his men were taking their ease and enjoying their pipes a large party of Indians that had been watching for a favorable opportunity dashed in on them and stampeded and drove off nearly all his horses, leaving most of them flat afoot. Fortunately for them,

Colonel W. C. Dalrymple happened to be near by with a ranging-company. Being notified of Colonel Baylor's mishap he immediately started with a part of his men in pursuit of the Indians. They were soon overtaken, and after a running fight of about twelve miles Colonel Dalrymple and his men succeeded in recapturing nearly all the stolen horses. Two of the Indians were killed—none of the rangers were hurt. Colonel Baylor is an old Indian fighter but for once (and I believe the only time) he was caught napping. Colonel Dalrymple's services on this occasion were rendered just in the nick of time, for if the Indians had succeeded in getting away with Colonel Baylor's horses he and his men would have had a hard road to travel in getting back to the settlements. Both these well known gentlemen are still living, and though they are growing somewhat old, they are still hale and hearty and give promise of many years of usefulness to their country.

Chapter 4

More Murders in Parker County

1861

THE details of the following murders of Youngblood, Killen, Washington and Mrs. Brown, will be given substantially in the language as they appear in Smythe's Historical Sketch of Parker county, from which they are taken. In the spring of 1861, the Indians came upon William Youngblood and killed him. The day previous a party of Captain M. D. Tacket's rangers, composed of David Stinson, Bud Slover, John Slover, — Boyd, — McMahan and others, were out on a scout, and while feeding at noon, eleven Indians were discovered coming out of a deep ravine, twelve miles north of Jacksboro. The Indians attacked the rangers but were quickly repulsed with the loss of one, and serious injury to a second. They made off, hotly pursued by the rangers, but having better horses, of course made the quickest time, and escaped. The rangers were distanced; still they followed on all night, but could not find the objects of their search. Early in the morning William Youngblood was going into the woods close by his house to cut and split rails, and while there nine Indians surrounded the place, scalped and killed him. The same morning the rangers were reinforced by James Gilleland, Angie Price. Palmer and other citizens. They overtook the murderers and killed the leader, who had Youngblood's scalp in his shot pouch. The scalp was instantly taken to the deceased's late residence, and placed on his head a moment before he was lowered into the earthly receptacle of the dead.

In the summer of 1861, John Killen and William Washington, each about twenty-four years of age, who resided on Grindstone creek, were stock hunting, and while resting at noon, were pounced upon and a well directed arrow killed the former, and another badly wounded the latter.

During the same summer Mrs. John Brown was killed, and possibly by the same party of Indians. This lady also lived on Grindstone creek. She had twin babies and had started to visit a neighbor near by, she carrying one of the children, and a girl about grown (one of the accounts we have, say she was a daughter, but of this we are not positive) the other. On their way they were attacked by a party of Indians. The girl who had one of the children was some distance ahead, and had well nigh reached her destination. Mrs. Brown, at the sight of the savage monsters, in her fright, for the moment, apparently forgot that she was the mother of the two children and clasping the child she carried in her own arms, tightly to her bosom, she ran hastily back to the house, crying "they shan't have mine, they shan't have mine." She finally reached the house, but the Indians soon came up, scalped and killed her on the spot, but spared the child.

Chapter 5

Marion Tacket—Sarah Mathews.

1862

TACKET settled in Parker county at an early day, near the line of Jack county. In the spring of 1862, as he was hunting his stock one day on the range he was attacked by Indians. Seeing there was no chance of escape by flight he took a stand behind a sapling three or four inches in diameter and defended himself to the last.

At length, however, an arrow pierced his lungs and another struck him in the neck, severing the jugular vein. But before he fell, he discharged both his gun and sixshooter at his assailants and it is supposed that he killed and wounded several. The Indians seeing a son of Mr. Tacket approaching, and probably thinking that others were coming, gathered up their dead and wounded and fled. The sapling behind which Tacket had taken his stand was stuck full of arrows. The Indians were pursued for some distance but were not overtaken. On the trail the dead body of an Indian was found covered over with stones, proving that one at least had paid for Tacket's life with his own.

We are not positive as to this date, but think it was in the month of October of the same year that the Mathews's family were attacked by a party of Indians, who murdered Mathews and one of his daughters and took Mrs. Sarah Mathews and four or five of her children prisoners. These Indians killed and captured the family of Mr. Stovall in the same neighborhood while Mr. Stovall was absent from home. There were also two or three captives taken from another family, whose names we do not know.

The whole number taken from the three families amounted to ten. Among them were two women and three children. Mrs. Mathews states that after the Indians captured her they traveled for thirty-six hours without rest or food. She carried her young child the whole way on her arm until it was perfectly numb and dead to all feeling. When the Indians had arrived at a point where they thought they would be safe from pursuit they made a halt and tied their prisoners securely. From thence on and until they reached the Indian village, the captives suffered terribly from exposure and want of food, and the Indians told them all the time that they intended to kill all the men and sell the women and children. These captives were carried about from point to point, between the Rocky mountains and Kansas. Finally, in 1864, a treaty was made with the Indians by the government of the United States, and these captives, with others, were released. Mr. Stovall learning that his son had been delivered to the government agent sent his brother after him. The agent turned him over to him and also the other nine captives. They were in a destitute condition and five or six hundred miles from home, but the government kindly provided for their wants and they were soon restored to their friends and relatives.

Chapter 6

Murders in Parker County, 1863 - 1873

DURING the year 1863, several families were living in the valley of Patrick's creek, in Parker county, the Rev. John Hamilton among the number. He owned, in connection with his farm, a small tannery. On one occasion he sent his sons, William and Stewart Hamilton, out into the woods to collect material for tanning purposes. While thus engaged the two young men were attacked by Indians. The frightened boys attempted to escape by running, but they were soon overtaken, their bodies pierced full of arrows. They were both killed and scalped, and before leaving, the heartless savages cut off one of the ears of Stewart, together with a portion of his head. During the same day either this or another party of the same band killed Mrs. F. C. Brown, who resided some four miles from Hamilton's, while standing in the yard in front of her door. Mrs. Brown had two daughters, Sarah, aged sixteen, and a younger daughter, whose name we do not know, about fourteen years of age. Those two young ladies had been over to visit their neighbor, Mr. Gatling, and were returning home when the merciless red skins fell upon them and seriously wounded both the young ladies with arrows. The eldest daughter, Sarah, died shortly afterwards from the effects of her wounds, but the younger one finally recovered. In September of the following year, 1864, William (or John, we are not positive as to the given name, accounts vary) Berry was killed on Sanches creek.

Berry resided in eastern Texas for several years, and then moved to Parker county, where he settled at what was known as the "Horse Shoe Bend." One day in the above named month, Berry and his little son went with a wagon to a field he had on the opposite side of the Brazos river for a load of pumpkins. When he started his wife insisted that he should take his gun with him, but he did not do so, thinking there was no danger, as no Indians had been seen in that section for a long time. He crossed the river, loaded his wagon and was on his way home when he was attacked by Indians who had secreted themselves in some brush near the road side. As he passed by, they suddenly rose and fired a volley at the wagon. Berry was instantly killed and his little boy was wounded in several places with arrows. The Indians beat his head with clubs until they thought he was dead and then left. But the little fellow was found shortly afterwards and got well of his wounds.

Mrs. Jane Smith was a resident of Parker county, and was also killed about this time. One day in the fall of 1864, while Mr. Smith was absent in the Confederate army, Mrs. Smith discovered a party of Indians about three-quarters of a mile distant coming towards the house. A moment afterwards she saw that they were in pursuit of two boys, whom they soon overtook and killed. Mrs. Smith told her children to run as fast as they could to the house of a neighbor, and that she would follow them in a little while. She did so, but before she could reach the house the Indians came up with her and killed her, and also two of her daughters, whom she had just overtaken in their flight. Mrs. Smith had her infant in her arms, and her eldest daughter who was near, seeing her fall, ran up to her, took the infant from the arms of her dead mother, and fled with the remaining children to an old gun shop that fortunately happened to be very near. There were several old guns in the shop, and when the Indians approached it the children presented them through the windows. The Indians thinking no doubt there was a man in the house, fell back when they saw the muzzles of the guns protruding from the windows, and finally left without making an attack. They then went to the house of Mr. Smith and plundered it of its contents. A near neighbor of Mr. Smith, hearing an unusual noise about his premises, started out to ascertain the cause. He had gone but a short distance when he discovered the Indians, and knowing that in all probability they would attack his own house, he hastily ran back. As soon as he reached it, he told his wife and children to run to the woods and hide themselves, and he would remain at the house to draw the attention of the Indians to himself and thus give them time to escape. They did so, and a few moments afterwards the Indians came galloping up, and seeing the owner of the house standing in front of it, they at once charged upon him. He immediately ran in the house, took his stand in the door, and presented his gun. Seeing he was prepared to defend the premises, the Indians, after some consultation among themselves, evidently came to the conclusion that it would be a risky business to attack him, and rode off the way they had come.

About four miles from this house they stole a number of horses and took a woman prisoner. They were pursued by a party of Texans. The Texans knew a pass in the mountains through which they believed the Indians would go on their way out, and they succeeded in reaching it before the Indians. They secreted themselves in the pass, and a little while after dark the Indians came riding along, totally unsuspicious of danger. The Texans waited until they could see them distinctly, and then fired a volley at them, killing several and wounding others. At the report of the guns, the Indians' horses "stampeded," and the one the captured lady was riding threw her to the ground. She was but slightly hurt, however, and concealed herself behind a large rock to prevent being shot by the Texans. A few moments before she had been a hopeless prisoner in the hands of her savage captors, and one can imagine what must have been her joyful feelings when she found herself among her own people.

Mr. Coldiron resided near Van Buren, in Parker county. If we are not mistaken in the date, it was one morning in the fall of the same year that Mr. Coldiron sent his two children out, a son and daughter, in search of a yoke of oxen. Whilst the little girl and her brother were still in sight of the house, a party of Indians who were concealed in the vicinity, rushed upon them and took them prisoners. They took the children to the top of a neighboring mountain, where they remained a day or two and then went off. A company of citizens pursued them, who after following them about sixty miles, overtook them and at once attacked them. Whilst the fight was going on the two children jumped from the horses they were riding, climbed to the top of a big rock, and amid the yells of the Indians and the firing of guns, the little girl cried out *"Don't shoot us, we are white folks"*. One of the men seeing the little girl and thinking she was an Indian, fired both barrels of his shot gun at her, but fortunately did not hit her. This caused the little girl to cry out louder, *"Please don't shoot any more, we are white folks."* The man who had fired at her. discovered from her voice that she was not an Indian, and went to where she was before the Indians retreated; and thus probably prevented them from taking the children with them when they left. They were properly cared for and restored to their family.

Figure 6.1: DON'T SHOOT AT US WE ARE WHITE CHILDREN.

In the following year Henry Maxwell was killed near his place on the Brazos. Maxwell came from the State of Arkansas to Texas, in the year 1842, and settled in Collin county, where he resided for about ten years. He then removed to Parker county. In the year 1865, Maxwell and his son-in-law, Mr. Joice, went out on the range for the purpose of hunting and collecting stock. Maxwell was armed with a shot gun and Joice with a rifle. After they had gone some distance on the range they saw a party of Indians coming towards them, who evidently had not discovered them. Joice proposed that they should fire on them at once, but Maxwell, who, as we have said, was armed with a shot gun, thought it would be best to wait until they approached nearer. The Indians, however, who just then discovered them, cut their discussion short by giving the war whoop and charging upon them.

Maxwell and Joice stood their ground and fired several rounds at the Indians, but the Indians were more numerous than they supposed and they soon surrounded the two men. Seeing the great odds they had to contend with they endeavored to retreat to a better position than the one they occupied, but before they succeeded in reaching it an arrow struck Maxwell in the back, inflicting a mortal wound. Finding his strength was rapidly failing he told his son-in- law to save himself if he could, that he was unable to fight or retreat. Joice then put spurs to his horse and fled, leaving the poor man to be slain by the Indians. The Indians did not pursue Joice, and it is reasonable to suppose from this fact, and the number of shots he and Maxwell fired at them that several of their number had been killed and wounded.

Joice raised a party of men and as soon as possible returned. They found Maxwell still alive and they carried him home, but he died that same evening.

Hugh O. Blackwell was also slain by a party of Indians while returning from Jacksboro to his home on Rock creek. He was killed, scalped and his horse taken. A few years previous to this, the Indians made a raid in that section of country and captured a little boy of Mr. Blackwell's and a little girl of — Sullivan's. They then went to the house of Samuel Hartfield while he and his family and a number of other persons who were assisting them, were engaged in making syrup.

As soon as the Indians were discovered, the whites being unarmed, all fled to the house. One lady, who had a child in her arms, begged the others not to leave her, whereupon a gentleman ran to her assistance, took the child from her, and by doing so, enabled her to escape.

The Indians then unharnessed the horse that was working in the sugar mill and made off with him. After going about ten miles, the little girl they had captured becoming troublesome to them, they put her to death. Her body was found some days afterwards much decayed, but it was identified beyond all doubt. The little son of Blackwell was retained a captive for several years, after which he was purchased by an agent of the United States government at Fort Cobb and restored to his friends in Parker county.

In July, 1866, a party of whites, while out on the range near West Meek's prairie, encountered a band of Indians, when a severe contest ensued. In this fight A. J. Gorman was killed.

He had only returned home from the war about one month previous.

Among the pioneer settlers of Parker county was an old gentleman by the name of Leeper. He lived seven miles northwest of Weatherford. He was a man about seventy years of age, and was a farmer by occupation.

In the fall of 1866, while the old man was at work one day on his farm, he was suddenly fired upon by a party of Indians and instantly killed. They scalped the old man and retreated without venturing to make an attack on the house.

There were two brothers, Bohlen and James Savage, living in Parker county; the first named lived on Sanches creek, the latter on Patrick creek. In the month of November, 1866, while plowing in the field, Bohlen Savage was shot in the neck by an arrow before he was aware of the presence of Indians. He immediately broke for the house but was overtaken, scalped and killed in the presence of his young daughter, who went out to meet him. This little girl was taken captive and remained with the Indians until in 1868. She was recovered at the Fort Sill agency in exchange for a pony. The Indians having killed Bohlen they passed on to his brother's house, where they succeeded in killing him also. The murder was of the most brutal character. We have been informed that the Indians captured three children from these two families. The youngest son was turned loose in the woods to perish only a short distance from where it was captured. The little creature was found the same evening and taken care of. After traveling some distance the Indians murdered one of the other children, whose body was afterwards found and identified by its clothing, Several years ago the widows of the Savage brothers were still living in Parker county.

During the year 1867 Oliver Loving was killed out on the Pecos river. We record his death here, for at that time he was a citizen of Parker county, living in the town of Weatherford, where he was engaged in buying stock for Charles Goodnight to drive to the Territories.

In the year before mentioned, 1867, he and others started to Colorado with a large drove of cattle. They went on without any interruption for about three weeks, and until they had arrived near the line between Texas and New Mexico. Here they halted the cattle, and sent Loving and a one armed man, named Wilson, ahead to pick out a camping place for the night. They had just reached the Pecos river near Horsehead crossing, when they were attacked by twenty-five or thirty Indians.

Wilson, riding an excellent horse, fled and reached the camp in safety; but they cut off the retreat of Loving and forced him to the river's edge. Although one arm was broken by a shot, he plunged bravely into the river and remained in the water under cover of some bushes for several hours. As soon as night came, fearing to come out on the same side of the river, on account of the Indians, who were still searching for him; he swam the Pecos, and took his course towards Fort Sumner.

But weakened by his great loss of blood and stay in the river, he was unable to travel far. He lay down, and from exhaustion fell asleep. He was awakened by some Mexicans who were passing by with a train of wagons.

They took him to Fort Sumner and placed him in charge of a surgeon, but his wounded arm had swollen to such an extent that an artery burst and he bled to death.

Jacob Lopp was a native of the State of Missouri. After immigrating to Texas he lived in several counties, but finally made his permanent home in Parker county, where he was eventually killed. In the month of August, 1868, a daughter of Mr. Lopp rode off one day some distance to visit one of the neighbors, telling him she would be back at a certain time. As she did not return at the designated hour Lopp became alarmed for her safety, and not waiting to get his horse, or his arms, he set out on foot in search of her. The old man had not gone more than half a mile from the house, when a party of Indians rushed upon him just as his daughter made her appearance in the road beyond. The Indians killed the old man in full view of his daughter, who was compelled to witness the terrible sight. Seeing there was no chance to get home, the young lady wheeled her horse and fled for life in the direction she had come, and succeeded in making her escape. It is thought the Indians did not discover her approach, as no attempt was made to pursue and capture her.

In the latter part of the same year Edward Rippey and his wife were both murdered at his residence. Rippey was a native of Tennessee, and had been in Texas but a short time. He was living fourteen miles west of Weatherford. On Christmas day, 1868, he and his wife were rendering lard in their kitchen, forty or fifty yards from the residence. Rippey seeing his dog baying something through the fence one hundred and fifty yards away, took his gun and started out, supposing it to be a varmint. He was almost there when the Indians, which it proved to be, fired upon him. Mrs. Rippey seeing her husband was wounded, took a gun and ran to his side. The fence protected the Indians from the bullets, and in a few moments Rippey and his wife were both killed. The children left the kitchen and ran to the house. An old rusty shot gun remained, and the oldest child taking it presented it at the door. The Indians having been taught some very dear lessons in that section of country, did not dare to approach the house. They plundered the kitchen, took the scalps of Rippey and wife and departed, soon followed by a posse of blood thirsty citizens.

Miss Rippey, a few years ago, was living with her grand father in Tarrant county. A few years prior to this sad event, Rippey's first wife came near being killed near the scene of this terrible tragedy. While carrying dinner to her husband and a lot of hired men, she was attacked by a party of Indians who chased her until she came to a grove of trees near where the men were at work. Here she stopped and threw her gun down on the Indians, but reserved the fire. After all attempts to get Mrs. Rippey to leave her position had failed, the cowardly savages withdrew.

The year following—1869—James Light and wife were scalped and left for dead while returning home from a neighbor's house where they had been passing a pleasant day on the fourth of July. They had two children with them, one was killed, while the other managed to escape during the confusion and hid in a thicket near by.

On Sunday morning, April 23, 1871, Linn Boyd Cranfill, a lad some fifteen years of age, was massacred by the Indians. He was the son of Isham Cranfill, who resided some twelve or thirteen miles from Weatherford. Linn had two favorite ponies, and bestowed upon them much of his time in seeing that they were properly cared for. On the ill-fated morning, says Mr. Smythe, whose narrative we substantially adopt, he arose unusually early and started out for his ponies. He was unarmed, a thing that had possibly never before happened since he was old enough to carry a revolver. While passing along the prairie looking for the objects of his search, and still within sight of his home, a party of Indians suddenly rushed upon him, shot him down and galloped away. An elder sister witnessed the bloody murder of her brother, and gave the alarm before the miserable wretches had time to scalp him. They were pursued for several miles, but, as was too frequently the case, were not overtaken. The lad lingered until the next day, when death came and relieved him of his sufferings. This is but one of the many instances where the youth of our border fell at the hands of the murderous savages, while just budding into manhood. Those who enjoy the peace and blessings civilization brings, have but a poor conception of the trying scenes through which the early settlers of the northwestern border passed, even as late as the period of which we are now writing. While the larger portion of the State was entirely free from the prowling bands of savages, yet they kept up their periodical raids, stealing horses and murdering people all along the northwestern border for several years.

The year following the murder of young Cranfill. They came across Thomas Landrum and shot and killed him while un-hitching a span of horses in front of Fuller Millsap's residence, on Rock creek. This was on the morning of March 14, 1872. Mr. Millsap and Joseph B. Loving seized their rifles, followed the miscreants, who were on foot, and killed one. Miss Donnie Millsap, a regular heroine, ran after her father with ammunition and was shot through her clothing several times, but fortunately without serious consequences. The Indians dragged off their dead companion and made good their escape. The young lady above mentioned (Miss Donnie Millsap) deserves more than a passing notice, and her many deeds of valor should some day be recorded by one more familiar with her thrilling adventures of frontier life, in order that the ladies of to-day might see what a conspicuous part their sex took in rescuing the northwestern border from the hands of the savage Comanche, and putting it in line with her sister counties in the front ranks of civilization. On several occasions Donnie Millsap helped to defend the homestead during the Indian raids in that section of country. Her father had but little fear of the hostile fiends, and the daughter seems to have inherited in a large degree the cool and daring bravery which was so characteristic of the father. Several years previous to the event which we have just related (we think it was in June, 1866) Mr. Millsap was engaged in a sharp conflict with two Indians when his daughter, Donnie, ran to him with some ammunition, whereupon the old gentleman spoke sharp to her and said: "For God's sake, Donnie, stay in the house, I'll manage this party." Upon this occasion the Indians were armed with bows and arrows, but when they killed Landrum, several years later, they were armed with improved firearms, and the services of Donnie were not so easily dispensed with by the old gentleman as upon the former occasion. Miss Millsap afterwards became the wife of Jesse Hitson, who, we think, in 1887, was living in Colorado City, Mitchell county, and is well known to the stockmen of northwest Texas.

A few months after the killing of Thomas Landrom, Jackson Hale and Martin Cathy were most foully murdered. These two youths, aged respectively thirteen and eighteen, the first named a son, and the latter a nephew, of Jesse Hale, had been to the town of Weatherford on the fourth of July to attend a circus.

In order to combine business with pleasure they took a wagon load of grain with them to have it ground. After seeing the show, they started in their wagon to return home. They were going along totally unsuspicious of danger, when a party of Indians rushed upon them from an ambuscade. The boys were unarmed and, of course, could make no resistance. The Indians shot them with arrows and thrust them through in many places with their spears.

When their bodies were found it was almost impossible to identify them, so terribly were they disfigured by wounds. One year afterwards the harness cut from the horses was found hanging to a tree two miles distant from the scene of the murder.

Some thirteen months later, John Hemphill was killed. This young man was a native Texan—a citizen of Parker county, and was born near the spot where he was killed. In the month of August, 1873, Hemphill, in company with several others, went one Sabbath to a church some distance from where they resided. As the moon shone brightly they postponed their departure until night. They had traveled but a short distance, when they discovered some people riding ahead of them. Supposing them to be some of their neighbors returning home from church, they spurred up their horses with the intention of overtaking them.

The people they had seen, however, were a party of Indians, who, no doubt, comprehending their mistake, rode rapidly on until they were hidden from view by a turn in the road, when they secreted themselves in some bushes near it, and awaited the approach of the young men. As they rode by totally unsuspicious of danger, the Indians fired upon them, and killed young Hemphill, but his companions were unhurt, and escaped. A company was raised the next day and the Indians were pursued for some distance, but they made good their escape.

This same party of Indians captured and carried off a large number of horses. During the same month George W. McClusky was killed while out in the yard, by an Indian who had crept up and concealed himself behind an oat stack. McCluskey lived with his father-in-law, John Baumgarner, and the two were walking around in the yard totally unsuspicious of danger, when McCluskey was shot and killed. The Indian then attempted to fire the oats but was prevented from doing so. This one instance illustrates the condition of affairs in the northwest, and the insecurity of human life, even as late as 1873. To those who are not familiar with the unsettled condition of Parker and adjoining counties at that time, such bold attacks in broad, open day light, in one's own premises, may seem somewhat incredulous, but nevertheless, they are true.

Chapter 7

Murders in Jack County

1859

IT will be remembered that the Indians commenced their depredations in Parker county during the year 1859, and so it was in Jack county. There was living in the above named county in 1859 a lady by the name of Mrs. Calhoun. She was the mother of six children and supported herself and family by her own exertions. In the spring of 1859, Mrs. Calhoun had been washing one day at a spring not far from the house and had left some articles of clothing there. She sent two of her children to get them, a lad about nine years old and a girl seven. As they did not return as soon as she expected she became alarmed and went out to look for them. Imagine the poor woman's horror when she discovered a party of Indians rapidly moving off from the spring. She ran to the place as fast as she could and called to her children, but receiving no answer and seeing nothing of them she hurried back to the house and dispatched one of her children to Jacksboro to tell the people that Indians had carried off a part of her family. A company of fifteen men was quickly raised. Six men from Johnson county joined them, making their total number twenty-one. They took the trail of the Indians, and after following it for about forty-five miles they came up with an old squaw, who was carrying the little girl on her back. She endeavored to hide in the brush, when she made such a desperate resistance that the enraged men killed her.

They then followed on the trail of the Indians who had possession of the little boy, and fifteen miles beyond they overtook them.

The whites charged on the Indians, who retreated as fast as they could, but the horses they were riding were pretty well broken down whilst those of the Texans were comparatively fresh, and they were soon overtaken. The Indians immediately abandoned their horses, and leaving them and the little boy, took to the brush for safety, where they scattered in every direction. Finding it impossible to follow their trail any longer, the Texans started for home, and it was not long until the two little children were soon presented to their distressed mother, who had given them up for lost.

We think it was during the same year, that the Indians attacked the house of Calvin Gage in his absence, killing Mrs. Gage and her infant, and Mrs. Katherine Saunders, mother-in-law of Gage. After committing these murders, the Indians then plundered the house and carried off such articles as they wanted. When they left, they took two daughters and a son of Gage prisoners. After traveling some fourteen miles with their prisoners, lashed fast on horses, they untied the little boy, and deliberately murdered him.

They then stripped the two girls of their clothing, and turned them loose to fare as best they could. These two girls wandered around in the woods for two days, exposed in their nude condition to all the inclemencies of weather and without a mouthful of food. The morning of the third day, they ascended a high hill, and from its top, to their great joy, they discovered a settlement about four miles distant. They directed their course towards it, and when they reached it, were kindly received by the people. They furnished them with clothing, and sent them home to their friends.

Chapter 8

Cameron and Mason Massacre

WILLIAM CAMERON was one of the early settlers in Texas—a farmer by occupation. His family consisted of himself, wife and five children. No other settlers being near, he and Mr. Mason built their houses close together for mutual protection. For some time they were very vigilant and cautious to guard against surprises by the Indians. But at length when no Indian "signs" had been seen in the vicinity for a long while they grew careless and pursued their daily avocations as if there were no danger to be apprehended.

In the spring of 1859, while Cameron and his son, a lad of some sixteen summers, were at work on the farm, the first intimation they had of danger was when they found themselves attacked by a large party of Indians. The father and son attempted to run to the house some three hundred yards away, but were shot down before they had proceeded far.

Mrs. Cameron, seeing from the house the perilous condition of her husband and that he was attempting to reach the house, seized a six shooter in one hand and her baby in the other with the intention of going to him, but finding the weapon unloaded she turned back and attempted to conceal herself in the cow lot. But the Indians had discovered and followed her. They treated her in a most brutal manner, splitting her head open with an ax, but left the little child beside her unharmed.

Cameron's other little son, witnessing the tragedy, started to the house of Mr. Mason, screaming loudly as he went. Mason, hearing his screams, took up his gun and ran towards the child, but before he could reach the lad the Indians had overtaken him, speared him and left him for dead. Mason made several attempts to shoot at the Indians, but his gun was out of order and failed to fire. Mrs. Mason, seeing that her husband's gun had failed to fire, ran towards him with a box of caps, but before she could reach him he was dead and scalped, and a few moments afterwards she and her little two year old child were also killed. Having ransacked both houses they left, taking with them one of Mrs. Cameron's children. A little girl of six and the baby two years of age they left unmolested, a thing very unusual. The little boy, whom they had left for dead, reviving, glanced at the horror spread around him and then started to the town of Jacksboro, ten miles distant, to carry the news, but he could not go more than a mile owing to his weakness, where he sat down by the root of a large tree and died.

The Indians, on their retreat, met a party of Californians, who, seeing they had a white child prisoner, determined to rescue it. The child was tied on a horse behind one of the Indians. The horses of the Californians being fresh, and those of the Indians pretty well broken down, they were coming up with them rapidly, when the Indian, behind whom the child was tied, cut it loose and let it drop to the ground. The child was unhurt, and the Californians, having gained the object of their pursuit, did not follow the Indians further. This child was the one they had stolen from Mrs. Cameron.

But now to return to the first portion of our story. The bodies of Mrs. Cameron and Mrs. Mason, as well as those of the others killed by the Indians, remained unburied and undiscovered for two or more days. A Mr. Flint, who happened to be passing Cameron's house, seeing no one about, went in and found the little girl sitting on the bed crying. The little creature was nearly starved, and could give no information as to what had become of the rest of the family. The baby, by the side of its dead mother in the cow lot, hearing Mr. Flint talking to the child in the house, cried aloud for assistance, lifting up her hands in piteous appeal, but would not leave the decaying body of her mother. Neither child had tasted food for three days. They were taken care of and the bodies of the unfortunate persons buried. These two families, living as they did, five or six miles from any other, will account for the fact that their deplorable condition was not discovered sooner. Both the fathers and mothers of these two families were slain, also two sons, and a baby girl taken captive, and the remaining two left to perish of hunger. As Cameron had twelve hundred dollars in his house, and many bad men were in the country, it is supposed the Indians were incited and assisted in the deed by them.

There was a family by the name of Willis, whose reputation was anything but a savory one. There were six or seven grown men in this family, and from the reputation they bore in the community in which they lived, it seems that there was no crime too heinous for them to commit. In one account which has been furnished us, this family is charged with being wholly responsible for the Cameron and Mason tragedy. Their connection with it is explained about as follows: It seems that the Willises in some way had ascertained the fact that there was a considerable amount of money stored away in the house of one of these families, and in order to get possession of it, they went to a camp of Comanche Indians and persuaded them to assist in the proposed robbery and murder of these two families. As this was strictly in the line of Comanche business but little persuasion was necessary to induce them to aid in any scheme of which murder and robbery was the object. The account we have, which connects the Willises with the massacre, states a little girl some eight years old, a daughter of one of the families, witnessed the whole proceedings. She had concealed herself when the Indians made the attack and thus escaped death. She states that when the attack was made on the house in which the money was stored away for safe keeping, a white man broke open the trunk and took the money out. When this terrible massacre became known, some of the exasperated citizens collected together, arrested a party of these scoundrels and gave them a trial, so the story goes, in Judge Lynch's Court. But, for once it would seem, the judge leaned a little too much to mercy's side. When the prisoners were arraigned, the little girl who had witnessed the horrible tragedy was brought forward as a witness. She stated that it was a man with red hair and a sandy beard who had killed her mother, and that the Indians killed the rest of the family. She also stated that she could recognize this man if he were brought before her. The little girl was then taken to the examining committee, and every one of the prisoners who, in any way, corresponded with the description given by the child was brought before her, one at a time. The moment Bill Willis was brought in, she immediately sprang up, and pointing to him, exclaimed: "That is the man who killed ma, and took pa's money from the trunk; but the Indians killed all the rest." Notwithstanding this strong evidence, these demons, for some unknown reason, were turned loose to continue their fiendish course of murder and robbery. But, although "the mills of the Gods grind slowly, they grind exceeding small," and their day of retribution came at last— at least to a portion of them. Subsequently the Willises stole a large number of horses, ran them to Mexico and sold them there. This was during the latter part of the war between the States. During the rebellion they were looked upon as traitors to their country, and were being watched for by the officers of the different counties. In attempting to pass back through the western portion of the State to their home in the northwest, they were arrested by a party, several miles above the city of Austin, brought to the capital of the State, and without court or jury, three of them were lynched by a vigilance committee. Many of the old citizens of Austin well remember the finale of the Willis brothers, and for aught we know, there may be some yet alive of the old residents of the city who could tell, if they would, the full particulars of the last moments spent on this earth by these assassins.

Chapter 9

Murders in Jack County, 1864 - 1874

WHILE Jack county suffered as much as most of her sister counties from frequent raids of the Indians, yet, comparatively speaking, we have but very few accounts of murders occurring in that county. The first on the list of which we have any account as having occurred in 1864 is that of John Reasnor. He first settled in Palo Pinto county, remained there some three years and then moved to Jack county, where he lived until he was murdered by the Indians in 1864.

Jack county is situated high upon the Brazos river, and at the time Mr. Reasnor moved into it, was subject to frequent incursions of the Indians. It was at a time, too, when the late civil war was raging between the two sections in the United States, and the frontiers were but poorly defended, as most of the men fit for service were absent in the army. Mr. Reasnor, in company with his little son, was at work on his farm when a party of about fifty Indians, who had approached under cover of some thick bushes, suddenly rushed upon them. Reasnor discovered the Indians before they reached him and he and his little son endeavored to save themselves by flight. Finding that the Indians were about to overtake them Reasnor ran in among some wheat stacks and hid himself, but they soon found him and put him to death with their spears. His little son, who was more active, succeeded in making his escape to the house, and the Indians left without venturing to attack it.

Some two years later the McKinney family were all murdered by the Indians. This family consisted of husband, wife and three children.

In the spring of 1866 he and his family went to visit some of their friends in Tarrant county. On their way home, it seems, they took a wrong road—one that had been but little traveled —and as they approached a deserted house, they were attacked by Indians. It was evident that the Indians had frightened the oxen so badly that they ran away, and threw the occupants out of the wagon. From all appearances the family were murdered as follows: McKinney took his youngest child, an infant, in his arms, and ran to a deep ravine. But the Indians followed him, and beat him to death with sticks. They then took the infant by the heels and knocked its brains out against a tree. After treating Mrs. McKinney in the most shameful manner, they thrust a spear through her heart, stripped her of her clothing, and scalped her. They killed one of the remaining children and took the other prisoner, but after going several miles they killed it also—thus exterminating the whole family.

We are not advised of the date of the attack on Francis M. Long, nor are we sure that it happened in Jack county, but we will record it here. Mr. Long was a native of Missouri. His parents emigrated to Texas in 1865, and settled in Montague county. Young Long was employed by some United States soldiers to pilot them from Elm creek, in Montague county, to Jacksboro, in Jack county. On his return home, he was discovered by a party of Comanches, who, finding he was alone, immediately gave chase to him. After they had run him about four miles, they succeeded in shooting him through the leg with an arrow, which also wounded his horse severely. Finding his horse was about to fail, young Long dismounted and ran into some thick brush near by. There he took his stand, and fought the Indians until he had emptied his Spencer rifle and two six-shooters at the redskins. The Indians were in open ground, and his shots told with deadly effect. They killed his wounded horse, but concluded, after all, they did not want his scalp, so they left it where it belonged, on the top of his head, and took their departure. Mr. Long suffered a great deal from his wound—had to lay out all night, and walk eight or ten miles the next day before he came to a settlement, but eventually he recovered.

During the year 1871 Charles E. Rivers was killed while gathering stock. Mr. Rivers was a native of Louisiana. His father came to Texas when Charles was but a child. After this young man grew to manhood, he moved to northwestern Texas, where he married the daughter of Mr. Loving. [Note. We are not positive, but think it was a daughter of Oliver Loving, who was killed by the Indians on the Pecos, and whose death we have recorded in the list of Parker county murders.] He engaged in the stock business and was quite successful. He made a contract in 1871 to furnish a large amount of beeves to a company. He was busily engaged in June, 1871, with his herders in gathering stock in Jack county, when he was attacked by a party of Indians.

They fired on his camp, mortally wounding Mr. Rivers. There were more men in the camp than it seems the Indians had supposed; and upon the discovery of this fact they retreated, after having fired, as above stated. As they left they ran through a large herd of horses and mules, causing them to stampede, and succeeded in carrying off some fifty head. Mr. Rivers being a man of fine constitution, lived over a month before he died. Strong hopes were entertained of his recovery, but the wound was too fatal. He had been of great service to the frontier, and was beloved by all who knew him. His widow still resided in the town of Weatherford, in Parker county, several years ago, so the writer was informed.

During the year 1873, the Indians were constantly raiding into Jack county, stealing horses, committing murders and creating terror wherever they went. Not unfrequently, herders upon the range were chased into camp, often barely escaping death at the hands of the pursuing savages. In the month of October, H. Walker and his son were both killed on the Salt fork of Keechi. We are not in possession, however, of the particulars of the killing.

During the month of November of the same year, the Indians killed Harris on the main fork of Keechi. Sorry we are not able to give full particulars in this instance also.

James R. Wright, an employee of J. C. Loving, was killed during the year 1874. Wright was a native of Arkansas. He came to Texas and settled in Loss valley, near the line of Young and Jack counties. He was employed by James C. Loving to assist him in managing his stock. Being an efficient herder and one that could be relied upon, Loving gave him full charge of his large stock and control of his hands. In taking care of so large a stock it often became necessary for the herders to separate and the Indians now and then took advantage of the opportunity thus offered them to add to their stock of scalps.

On the twentieth day of May, 1874, Wright, when at some distance from his men, was suddenly attacked by a party of Indians. When he discovered them they had almost surrounded him, leaving him but a little chance to escape. He was mounted upon a good horse and started towards his men, but, unfortunately, in attempting to leap a gully the animal fell and threw him. He attempted to remount and had just succeeded in doing so when the Indians fired upon him at close quarters, killing him instantly. They took his horse and arms and the much coveted scalp and left for the mountains.

John H. Heath, who was also an employee of J.C. Loving, was killed on the tenth day of July following. Heath first settled in Parker county and subsequently was employed by James Loving to herd horses in Jack county. These horses were, of course, an inducement to the Indians to frequent the locality where they were pastured. Heath, in company with other herders, went out upon the range one day in the month of July, 1874 for the purpose of driving the stock to his ranch. After he had collected the herd he drove it to the ranch and was just in the act of penning them when a party of Indians made a furious attack upon him. At their first fire Heath fell dead with a bullet through his brain.

There were several men in the ranch at the time, who flew to their arms and a fight ensued, lasting for an hour or more. Finding the Texans were too much for them they retreated, and as they carried off their dead and wounded, it was not known what loss they had sustained. None of the Texans except Heath were killed in this fight. About the same time the Indians stole two hundred head of horses and mules from Hensley, Cooper, Lindsey and Rogers.

Chapter 10

The Tacket Fight—Young County

1859

THE first pioneer preacher in Young county was Old Father Tacket, as he was familiarly called. He was of the Methodist creed. He moved his family on Boggy creek, in the western portion of Young county. On the fifteenth of January, 1859, about ten o'clock in the morning, one of his cows came up alone. He thought it strange that she would leave the bunch, and, upon examination, found an arrow sticking in her neck.

He and his three sons, Jim, George and Lycurgus, arming themselves, each, with a shotgun and six-shooter, took the back trail of the wounded cow, which they could easily follow, as the snow lay on the ground to the depth of several inches. They followed the trail for about two miles, where they found the remainder of the heard at the foot of a very rough hill, to which the present occurrence gave the name of "Tacket Mountain." Not daring to follow the redskins into such a place, they rounded up their little bunch of cattle and started for home. The Indians, observing them from the summit of the mountain, concealed themselves in a deep gulch which headed there, and, running to where the path crossed it, they lay in ambush for their approach. The cattle became frightened at the crossing, and Lycurgus, thinking some wild animal was Crouched there, cocked and presented his gun. At this moment the Indians sprang up, and Lycurgus shot the only one who had a gun. Eleven Indians more were left, and a general fight ensued. The Indians thought the Tackets were only armed with guns, and when they had emptied them, the blood thirsty demons threw down their bows, leaped from out the gully, knives in hand, to make a charge for scalps. The pistols were then, for the first time, drawn, and with deadly effect. The Indians fled in great confusion, leaving four of their dead on the field of battle. Father Tacket and son Jim were wounded slightly— in the foot and eyebrow, respectively. They did not follow up their advantage and exterminate the whole marauding band, but returned home, without being further molested.

The old man lived in Young county until 1883, when he moved to Parker county, and in 1887 he died. Jim Tacket now has a large cattle ranch in the Texas Panhandle.

A party in the spring of 1860, left Fort Belknap and the settlements close by, to gather cattle on Elm Creek. One day when they had been out about a week, on the thirtieth of April, Newhouse and a Mexican, who were in the company, were left on herd. The others were at their dinner, when a small band of Indians attacked Newhouse and the Mexican. They made fight but to no avail. Both men were killed, and although pursued by the remainder of the party, the Indians made good their escape.

In the summer of 1861, a man by the name of Butoff, left his "clearing" on Elm Creek, in Young county, with a hide press, taking it to Johnson county. Butoff was driving four yoke of oxen, and had proceeded about thirty-five miles on his way, to what is now called Dillingham prairie. He was here riding on the tongue of his wagon, wholly unsuspicious of danger, when a party of six Indians came upon him from behind and killed him. A Mr. Glasinjim who was horse hunting on the range, seeing the man was unconscious of his danger, and thinking he would find a gun at the wagon, put spurs to his mule, intending to reach the spot before the Indians. The Indians rode fleet horses, and his mule was so slow that he found this impossible, so he faced about, thinking to reach his home on Rock Creek, a mile and a half distant. The Indians, after they had murdered Butoff, gave chase. They came within arrow shot of him when in about half a mile of his house. Seeing they would soon overtake and slaughter him, he concluded to sell his life as dearly as possible, so he drew his revolver and faced them, cursing them with every breath. They stopped, laughed at his pluck and impudence, held a consultation, and retraced their steps to plunder the wagon of the murdered man.

Some two years later three Indians were killed in an engagement with Texas rangers.

In the fall of 1863 a party of rangers belonging to Captain White's company, Colonel McCord's regiment, started to carry an express from Loss Valley to Fort Belknap. On their way they came across four Indians. A man named Jim Dozier fired and killed one of the Indians. Whilst he was reloading his gun the rest of the party, six or seven in number, continued the fight with their six shooters, as they had no guns, but failed to do any damage to the enemy. As soon as Mr. Dozier had reloaded his gun he fired again and killed another Indian. The two remaining Indians then fled, and the men with six shooters pursued them. They finally succeeded, after much firing, in killing one of them, but the other escaped. Mr. Dozier killed two Indians with his rifle, whilst the rest of the party only killed one, which clearly proves the superiority of the rifle to the six shooter, especially when in the hands of such an experienced frontiersman and Indian fighter as Dozier.

The sad death of Alf. Lane occurred the following year, which happened under peculiar circumstances. In the month of July, 1864, Goodnight removed a bunch of cattle from Keechi Valley, going with them to the territories. On the second night of their drive, they camped at a place known as Fort Murray, in Young county. In the company was a young man, Alf. Lane, a brother-in-law of Mr. Goodnight. While in camp here at Fort Murray, Lane dreamed that his father and mother, whom he had left at their home on Keechi creek, had been massacred by the Indians, and it appeared to him so vividly that he determined to leave the trail and return. Goodnight reasoned with him, told him how hazardous the attempt, and how foolish his apprehensions. But no, he must go; nothing would satisfy him short of going back to see.

Alas, his vision leads him to his doom! He had gone only some six or eight miles on his return, when he was killed by a band of marauding Indians. When found his body was at the foot of the Cement mountain, ten miles north of the town of Graham, horribly mangled, as though the killing was not enough, but torture had to be resorted to, to satisfy their vicious cravings.

Chapter 11

Peveler and Cox

1864

CAPTAIN PEVELER was a native of the State of Kentucky. On his arrival in Texas he settled at Fort Belknap in Young county. Some time afterwards he was elected captain of the militia. His name was a terror to the red skin race, and well they knew that they could not commit their depredations in reach of him with impunity. In September, 1864, he, in company with State Cox (who was then sheriff of Young county), Cole Duncan, Perry Harmison and George Hunter, went over to Loss valley, in Jack county, to the annual round up.

They had proceeded on their homeward journey to a spot about ten miles north of the town of Graham, driving a small bunch of cattle, when they saw a band of six or eight Indians ahead and gave chase. They followed them into a dense mesquite thicket and here, as if by magic, fifty or sixty Indians sprang up around them. They would have immediately retreated had not the horse which Cox was riding been unable to run. They all dismounted, determined to share the fate of Cox, be it for weal or for woe. Cox pleaded so piteously for them to save their own lives and let him take his chances that at last a retreat was ordered. It seems that Cox became excited, for he mounted his horse without untying him from the tree and starting off at full speed, the jerk of the rope broke his horse's neck. After falling from his horse he was soon dispatched. Harmison, Duncan and Hunter, who were unhurt when the retreat was ordered, fled precipitately and never halted until they were inside the walls of Fort Belknap, where they reported that the Captain and Cox had been killed. Peveler, however, having received a number of wounds, was much weakened by loss of blood, and his horse also being badly wounded he was compelled to move slowly. He had gone only a few hundred yards and reached a deep ravine when they had almost overtaken him. There was only one crossing to this ravine, which was a narrow path and very deep. Peveler had just crossed over and was ascending the other bank when the howling pack of Indians, headed by their chief, came rushing on him. Just as the chief reached the bottom of the canon, Peveler, seeing his opportunity, shot him dead from his horse. He fell square in the path and not a horse could be-urged over the dead body. The Indians, unwilling to leave their horses, held a war dance over the remains of their chieftain and left for parts unknown. Captain Peveler, wounded as he was, and riding a wounded horse, rode eight miles with an arrow sticking in his neck. On arriving at the house of a Mr. Crossman the arrow was extracted with great difficulty, and, notwithstanding he was suffering with no less than sixteen wounds, he lived for fifteen days. These men, expecting no such trouble, were armed only with sixshooters, but with these feeble weapons several Indians were left dead upon the battle ground and many more wounded. A hill near where the occurrence took place now bears the name of Cox mountain, an undecaying monument to the memory of State Cox.

James McCoy and his son were both slain by a prowling band of savages the same year. McCoy came from Missouri to Texas and settled in Hood county. In 1863 he moved to the vicinity of Fort Belknap. On the thirteenth of October, 1864, whilst he and his son were engaged in hauling rails to fence a farm, they were charged upon by a party of Indians. These Indians had just come out of a fight with some State rangers, in which they had got the best of the soldiers. Flushed with their victory, and falling in shortly afterwards with McCoy and his son, they at once attacked them. The rangers, who were still in sight, saw the Indians attack McCoy and son, and knowing it was impossible to aid them, they did the next best thing they could do, hurried to his house took Mrs. McCoy and her niece behind them on their horses, and carried them to Fort Belknap —thereby saving them from death or captivity. McCoy and his son were both killed.

In 1867 a triple massacre occurred near Belknap—Proffitt, Johnson and Carlton, in July, 1867, while branding cattle near Fort Belknap, in Young county, were surprised by a horde of savages. Their Winchesters were on their saddles, and they had, as usual, turned their horses, loose to graze. The animals had wandered off some distance from the lot. In attempting to reach the horses all the men were killed. The Proffitt killed in this massacre was a brother to John Proffitt, now, in 1888, a popular ranch man in Young county.

In the fall of the year, 1868, a herdsman for Charles Rivers was out with his stock on Salt Creek prairie, about two miles from camp. He was attacked by several Indians, and for nearly a mile kept them off in a running fight, himself on foot, and with no weapon but his six shooter. Weakened by loss of blood from his wounds, he could run no further, and sank down exhausted. They ran to him, fractured his skull with a club, scalped him, and left him for dead. Soon after they left him he revived, walked a mile to camp, and lived for six days. He was shot three times, his skull fractured, and was then scalped. It was thought that, had not the "screw worms" eaten into his brain, he would have recovered from his wounds.

Chapter 12

Rock Creek Fight

1871

ON Sunday the sixteenth day of April, 1871, near Rock creek, and close to the line between Young and Palo Pinto counties, and not a great distance from Fort Belknap, occurred one of the most desperate and bloody fights that ever occurred on the northwestern border. We are sorry that we are not in possession of the names of all the twelve men who made such a gallant stand against such an overwhelming force of well armed Indian warriors, and that we have thus far obtained only a meagre account of the particulars of this bloody encounter. During the month of April in the year above named, the stock men of Palo Pinto and adjoining counties were engaged in their annual spring "round up," when a party of twelve men were attacked by about forty or fifty armed Indian warriors. We have the names of only a few of the whites who participated in the engagement, and they are as follows: Jason McLean, who lived on Keechi creek, in Palo Pinto county; I. E. Graves, who, in 1888, lived in Weatherford, Parker county; George and John Lemley who resided, we believe, in either Palo Pinto or Parker county; Shap Carter and Tom Crow. The country where they were attacked was a level prairie, and the Texans took their position in a shallow ravine to defend themselves against the great odds they had to contend with. The ravine proved to be too shallow to afford them much protection, and they were greatly exposed to the constant fire the Indians poured upon them.

It appears that the chief in command of the Indians on this occasion directed the movements of his warriors through a negro. The chief took his position about two hundred yards in the rear of the Indian lines, on an eminence, from whence he could overlook the position held by the Texans, and every movement they made was communicated through couriers to the negro who was in command of the fight. The Texans had no arms but six shooters, and the Indians' long range guns gave them a great advantage. Eight of the horses ridden by the Texans were shot down in the beginning of the fight. This was a bloody day to these beleaguered Texans. As they were but poorly protected from the bullets of the enemy they suffered severely.

Late in the evening, the Indians, unaware of the damage inflicted upon the Texans, withdrew, taking with them all the horses belonging to the Texans, and a large portion of the cattle. Eight out of the twelve Texans were either killed or wounded in this fight. Tom Crow was killed dead on the ground (whereupon the Indians cried out "Wano!") and two of the wounded died shortly afterwards. The day following John Lemley died, and the next day Shap Carter died. If the Indians had known that there were but four men among the Texans not wounded, they, no doubt, would have attacked them again, and it is probable they would have discovered the fact had it not been for one of the party, Mr. Graves. When the Indians withdrew from the field, they ascended an eminence beyond gun shot, from whence they could plainly see the Texans in the shallow ravine. Graves made all the men, who were able to do so, stand up, thereby making the Indians believe they had suffered but little damage. This little piece of stratagem no doubt saved the lives of the few who thus far had survived this terrible conflict. George Lemley, who now—1888—lives near the place where the fight occurred, bears an ugly scar on his cheek to remind him of that direful day.

In the month of May following the Rock Creek fight, Henry H. Helerin was murdered in a most brutal manner. Mr. Helerin, previous to his coming to Texas, had been a great traveler, rambling about over the world. He became tired of traveling, and came to Texas for the purpose of going into the stock business. He went to Parker county, and engaged to work with Mr. Charles E. Rivers, who was also killed in Jack county the following month. He was engaged as Mr. Rivers' book-keeper. He would often go out among the stock, and amuse himself looking at them. One day in the month of May, 1871, he took a long ride, and concluded to rest a while. He alighted from his horse and sat down at the root of a tree. While thus enjoying a rest, a party of Indians discovered him, slipped up to him, and shot him. After this they scalped him, and left him for dead. But he revived. He was perfectly conscious, and knew when they scalped him, but could do nothing. The herders, who were near by, heard the firing, and ran to see what was the matter; but they were too late. The bloody work had been done, and the Indians were gone. The young man lived for thirty-six hours after being scalped.

Chapter 13

Gen. W. T. Sherman's Tour of Inspection

1871

DURING the year 1871, General W. T. Sherman made a tour of inspection, which included the military posts in Texas. It was in the same year that Satanta and Big Tree made their famous raid in Northwest Texas, upon which occasion they attacked a wagon train belonging to Henry Warren, while en route on the military road leading from Jacksboro to Fort Griffin, in Shackelford county. The Indians killed seven out of the twelve teamsters, then fired the wagon train, with one of the teamsters chained to the wagon wheel, while yet alive, to be consumed amid the torturing flames. Five of the teamsters made their escape. The day previous to this fiendish massacre, General Sherman, with his escort, passed along the same road on his way to Fort Richardson, at Jacksboro. In 1877, when Mr. H. Smythe, of Weatherford, Parker county, was writing his little book entitled ''Historical Sketch of Parker County, Texas,'' General Sherman kindly furnished him with a manuscript copy of the journal kept on the general-in-chiefs tour of inspection, by Inspector General R. B. Marcy, during the months of April, May and June, 1871. From Mr. Smythe's book, we obtain the following data. Much of this journal relates to the attack on Warren's wagon train and massacre of the teamsters, the capture of the Chiefs Satanta, Big Tree and Satank, and the subsequent history of these noted chiefs; besides, the journal kept upon this occasion shows clearly the condition of our frontier settlements at that time, and coming from the general-in-chief of the United States army, can be taken as absolutely true.

General Sherman and party left New Orleans, April 18th, by rail to Lake Pontchertrain, and thence on the steam revenue vessel, "The Wilderness," for Mobile, arriving there on the afternoon of the nineteenth. April the 20th, they returned to New Orleans. While there General Sherman examined Forts Jackson and St. Philip; on the twenty-third the party left New Orleans for Brashear City, where the party embarked on one of Morgan's steamers for Galveston, reaching there at day break the following morning, and by rail arrived at Columbus at 6 p. m. They left Columbus on the twenty-fifth in a spring wagon, sent forward by the quarter master at San Antonio. On the twenty-seventh they arrived at Seguin, and on the following day arrived at San Antonio, and remained at that place—the headquarters of the department—until the morning of May the 2nd, dining with General Reynold on the twenty-ninth, and attending a ball in the evening, given by the German club.

From San Antonio, General Sherman and staff were accompanied by an escort of seventeen men of the Tenth Infantry and camped thirty miles from San Antonio on the evening of May 2. They passed through Boerne and on May 4 reached Fredericksburg. Passing on up the country through Fort Mason,

Menardville and Fort McKavett the party camped at Kickapoo Springs, in Concho county, on the ninth, and arrived at Fort Concho, in Tom Green county, May 10. From Fort Concho the party proceeded north, passing old Fort Chadborne, in Runnels county, on the twelfth, and on the following evening reached old Fort Phantom hill. May 14 brought the party to Fort Griffin, in Shackelford county, where they remained during the fifteenth, and on the sixteenth, Fort Belknap, in Young county), was entered. Here General Sherman ordered that a detachment of troops be sent to Fort Belknap from Fort Richardson for picket service, as the Indians came there often and troubled travelers and the two or three families that lived near the fort. On May 17, General Sherman's party set out for Fort Richardson, in Jack county. We now quote from the journal, which shows the condition of the country at that time. "We passed immense herds of cattle to-day, which are allowed to run wild upon the prairies and they multiply very rapidly. The only attention the owners give to them is to brand the calves and occasionally go out to see where they range. The remains of several ranches were observed, the occupants of which have either been killed or driven off to the more dense settlements by the Indians. Indeed, this rich and beautiful section does not contain today (May 17, 1871) as many white people as it did when I (General Marcy) visited it eighteen years ago, and if the Indian marauders are not punished the whole country seems to be in a fair way of becoming totally depopulated.

"May 18, 1871.—This morning five teamsters, who, with seven others, had been with a mule wagon train en route to Fort Griffin (Captain Henry Warren's) with corn for the post were attacked on the open prairie, about ten miles east of Salt creek, by one hundred Indians and seven of the teamsters were killed and one wounded. General Sherman immediately ordered

Colonel MacKenzie to take a force of one hundred and fifty cavalrymen with thirty day's rations on pack mules and pursue and chastise the murderers."

This brings us up to the date of the attack upon the wagon train; but before beginning the details of this tragedy we will follow General Sherman further on in his tour of inspection. On the nineteenth, General Sherman remained at Fort Richardson and received a delegation of gentlemen from Jack and Parker counties, among whom were W. W. Duke, R. J. Winders, J. R. Robinson, W. M. McConnell, Peter Hart and H. H, Gaines.

They represented the exact condition of affairs, growing out of the infamous and suicidal government policy of rewarding these savage brutes for murdering the whites, and assured him that unless decisive action was taken, and the Indians put down, that Northwest Texas would soon become depopulated, the labor and industry and accumulations of years would be lost, families scattered, important interests sacrificed, society ruined, and a delightful and improving country given over to the blight of these demons. General Sherman listened attentively and grasped the entire situation. He keenly felt the humiliation of the Indian policy of the United States, acknowledged its injustice, and promised to do all in his power to remedy the condition of affairs then existing. The deputation requested authority to go to Fort Sill to recover stock that had been stolen from them by the Indians, when General Sherman invited them to go with him the following day and identify their animals. During that day, Colonel Mackenzie reported that the information concerning the murder of the teamsters in Captain Henry Warren's train was correct; that their bodies were found much mutilated, and one of the Elliott brothers (Samuel) "burned to a cinder."

On the twentieth day of May, General Sherman's party left Jacksboro for Fort Sill, and on the twenty-first crossed Red River at Red River Station, the same being the great crossing for the herds of cattle going from Texas to Kansas. In the afternoon of the twenty-third they arrived at Fort Sill, where they changed their escort, and for the first time after leaving San Antonio, went into quarters. Fort Sill is situated on an elevated plateau, near the eastern extremity of the Wichita mountain, and upon the identical spot, says General Marcy, that he recommended for a military post in 1852. During the twenty-fourth and twenty-fifth, General Sherman remained at Fort Sill examining into the condition of affairs with General Grierson and others, and on the twenty-sixth visited the signal station, on one of the most easterly peaks of the Wichita mountains. But before following General Sherman further, let us now return to the operations of the three noted Kiowa chiefs while on their raids in Texas.

Chapter 14

Satanta, Satank and Big Tree's Raid

1871

THERE is no act of savage cruelty recorded in the history of our Indian warfare more barbarous and inhuman, than the unwarranted attack by one hundred and fifty warriors under the leadership of the three above named Kiowa chiefs upon Henry Warren's wagon train on the eighteenth day of May, 1871. Warren had a contract for freighting between Forts Richardson and Sill, and on the above named day, his mule wagon train, while freighting between these two forts was attacked by this prowling band of blood thirsty villains, just as the twelve teamsters were preparing to strike camp. The alarm of "Indians" was given by one of the teamsters, and the wagons were quickly corralled. A short and deadly fight ensued, in which seven of the twelve teamsters were killed and one wounded. The remaining four, together with the wounded teamster, fled to a point of timber close by, where they concealed themselves in the brush, thus narrowly escaping a cruel death, and finally made their way to Jacksboro. To-day, twelve miles northeast of Graham, the county seat of Young county, on or near the old military road leading from Jacksboro to Belknap and Fort Griffin, stands a monument erected to the memory of the seven teamsters who were so foully murdered on that sad day. The balance of the history pertaining to this monstrous outrage perpetrated by savage brutes will all be taken from Mr. Smythe's "Historical Sketch of Parker County."

The burning of the train and massacre of the teamsters must have occurred near the line between Young and Jack counties, but in the latter, as the chiefs were tried and convicted at Jacksboro.

"A MOST CONSPICUOUS YEAR WAS 1871."

During the months of that and the previous year, sad and serious consequences resulted to many persons in this vicinity. Murders were frequent, Indian massacres numerous and society in constant agitation. The whole frontier country was kept in a continual state of excitement and many settlers left for the east temporarily, while others actually returned to the States from whence they emigrated. It was a dark period for Western Texas, and the terrible tragedies enacted made warriors out of many men, women and children who, previously, were anything but adepts in the use of the revolver or the rifle. Tired of the many raids indulged in by the Comanches and the Kiowas, and sick of the consequences of those periodic visitations the people resolved upon action; but, early in the year, learning that General W. T. Sherman was about to visit Texas and make a tour of this frontier country determined to wait his presence. In the meantime other murders were perpetrated and life was considered unsafe, even one single mile from home, while property was at the mercy of these marauding parties. In addition to the several massacres, mentioned elsewhere, seven teamsters in the employ of Captain Henry Warren, on the road to Fort Griffin, were killed by a band of one hundred and fifty Kiowas, commanded by

SATANTA

The chief who signed the very treaty of peace (August, 1869), between his tribe and the United States, under which he and they were being fed and protected by the government, at the Fort Sill reservation. This was on the eighteenth day of May, 1871. The names of the unfortunate men were Nathaniel S. Long, wagon master of the train, John Mullens, James S. Elliot, Samuel Elliot, M. J. Baxter, and Jesse Bowman, teamsters from Clay county, Missouri, and James Williams, teamster from Eastern Texas. Thomas Brazeal, teamster, was seriously wounded, and R. A. Day and Charles Brady, teamster, escaped. [Note. The names of the other two teamsters who made their escape, and not mentioned by Mr. Smythe, were Hobbs Carey and Dick Motor.] This noted chief, Satanta, is described by W. E. Webb, in his "Buffalo Land," page 180, as "the very embodiment of treachery, ferocity and bravado. Phrenologically considered, his head must have been a cranial marvel, and the bump on it maping out the kingdom of evil, a sort of Rocky mountain chain, towering over the more peaceful valleys around. Viewed from the towering peaks of combativeness and acquisitiveness, the territory of his past would reveal to the phrenologist an untold number of government mules, fenced in by suttler's stores, while bending over the bloody trail leading back almost to his bark cradle, would be the shades of many mothers and wives, searching among the wrecks of emigrant trains for flesh of their flesh, and bone of their bone. Satanta was long a name on the plains to hate and abhor. He was an abject beggar in the pale face's camp, and a demon on their trail."

THE LAST DRAW

We left General Sherman and party at Fort Sill looking into the condition of affairs. We again quote from his journal:

"May 27.—This afternoon about four o'clock several Kiowa chiefs, among them Satanta, Satank, Kicking Bird and Lone Wolf, came to the agency to draw their rations. In a talk with Agent Tatem, Satanta said he with one hundred warriors, had made the recent attack upon the trains between Fort Richardson and Belknap; that they had killed seven teamsters and driven off forty-one mules. This he considered a meritorious exploit and said: "If any other Indian claimed the credit of it, he would be a liar that he was the man who commanded." He pointed out Satank, Big Tree and another chief as having been with him in the action. The agent immediately reported the facts to General Sherman and requested him to arrest the Indians concerned; whereupon the General sent for them and Satanta acknowledged what he had stated to the agent, when the General informed him that he would place them in confinement and send them to Texas for trial by the civil authorities. Satanta, seeing that he was likely to get into trouble, replied that, although he was present at the fight, he did not kill anybody himself, neither did he blow his bugle.

[Note by General Sherman.—The conversation with Satanta was through an interpreter. I understood him to say he took no part in the fight except to blow his trumpet. At that instant of time he had an ordinary trumpet slung on his person. —W. T. S.]

"His young men wanted to have a little fight and to take a few white scalps, and he was prevailed upon to go with them merely to show them how to make war, but that he stood back during the engagement and merely gave directions. He added that some time ago the whites had killed three of his people and wounded four more, so that this little affair made the account square, and that he was now ready to commence anew —cry quits. General Sherman told him it was a very cowardly thing for one hundred warriors to attack twelve poor teamsters who did not pretend to know how to fight. That if he desired to have a battle the soldiers were ready to meet him at any time. That he would send the three men (Indians implicated) to Texas for trial. Seeing no escape, Satanta remarked that rather than be sent to Texas he preferred being shot on the spot. About this time Kicking Bird arrived. He had seen the General on the Arkansas river. He is one of the most influential chiefs of his tribe and has generally behaved tolerably well. He arose and said that he, as General Grierson and the agent well know, had done everything in his power to prevent his young warriors from leaving the reservation and going to Texas for marauding purposes. That he had invariably endeavored to keep his followers in the right path, and for the sake of the good he had done he now asked the General to release his friends from arrest and he would return the captured mules. General Sherman replied that he fully appreciated all that he had done and that he, himself, would be kindly treated so long as he continued to do well, but that the arrested Indians must be sent to Texas.

"About twenty armed soldiers now came up in front of the piazza where we were assembled, and the Indians seemed quite excited, nearly every one of them having a Spencer carbine or a Colt's revolver. Kicking Bird continued in the endeavor to persuade the General to release the chiefs—said he was friendly to the whites, and should feel sorry if war ensued from this affair, but of course he should be with his people in the latter event. Another Indian named Lone Wolf also rode up upon a fine horse, dismounted, laid two Spencer carbines and a bow and quiver of arrows upon the ground, tied his horse to the fence, then throwing his blanket from his shoulder, fastened it around his waist, picked up the carbines in one hand and the bow and arrows in the other, and with the most deliberate and defiant air, strode up to the piazza, then giving one of his carbines to an Indian who had no arms, and the bow and arrows to another, who at once strung the bow and pulled out a handful of arrows, he seated himself and cocked his carbine —at which the soldiers all brought their carbines to an aim upon the crowd—whereupon Satanta and some other Indians held up their hands and cried, no! no! no! don't shoot! The soldiers were directed not to fire, but just at this moment we heard shots fired outside the fort, which resulted from the fact that the guard had been ordered to permit no Indians to leave without further instructions. Some Indians, in attempting to go out, had been halted by the sentinels, when one of them shot an arrow, wounding one of the sentinels. The shot was returned, killing the Indian as he was riding off. When the excitement had subsided a little, the General told the Indians that they must return the forty-one mules, which Kicking Bird promised to do, and he went off for them, but on his arrival at the camp he discovered that the squaws had become frightened and ran off with all their animals except eight, which were taken possession of. All the Indians were allowed to leave except the prisoners, who were put in irons and closely guarded. The benevolent, civilizing peace policy, so urgently advocated by a class of people in the eastern States, has received a long and fair experimental trial with these Indians. They have been regularly fed and the kindest treatment extended to them for two years by our authorities, but it has not had the slightest effect upon them. *They have no more conception of gratitude than so many wolves, and they have continually been stealing horses and mules, murdering men, ravishing women and enslaving children. Besides, they have not only openly acknowledged, but have boasted of these atrocities.* There was hardly a day during our trip through the frontier settlements of Texas that we did not hear of some persons who had suffered from Indian raids, and there seems to he no prospect of their ceasing.

"The question has resolved itself into this, *that the border settlers of Texas must all be annihilated, or the Indian chastised, and disarmed.* Many of them have the best modern arms, and they know how to use them well, which has given them confidence in their ability to cope with the whites in battle. While they were armed with bows and arrows only, they were comparatively powerless against equal numbers of white troops, but those officers who have encountered them recently, say they fight well, and do not care about meeting them again with any very great odds against them. The prairie Indians seldom ever uses fire arms in hunting; they kill the buffalo with the bow and arrow, and this is about the only animal they hunt. They reserve all their ammunition for war purposes, and it is a well known fact that they will sacrifice anything to get ammunition, moreover, they will not sell their fire arms at any price."

The agent, Tatum, in one of his interviews with General Sherman, remarked that he was glad the General happened here at this particular time, as it gave him an opportunity to witness the actual condition of Indian matters: that he not only approved the course pursued in arresting these Indians, but he would have been glad if Lone Wolf had been arrested, as he is one of the boldest and most troublesome men of his tribe.

"He also said that it had been, his opinion for a year that severe measures should be resorted to towards these Indians, and had so informed the Indian Bureau, but. that no attention had been paid to his representations. He concluded his remarks by saying that, if the Texas people followed Indians, who had stolen their stock, into the reservation, they would not be prevented by him. He is decidedly of the opinion that the Indians should be held to a strict accountability for all their misdeeds, and this sentiment is concurred in by every disinterested sensible man on the frontier."

As before stated, Satanta, Big Tree and Satank were arrested on May 27, at Fort Sill.

They were at once heavily ironed, and on the thirty-first, two of them were safely lodged in the jail at Jacksboro, by Colonel R. S. MacKenzie, under whose escort, with a detachment of soldiers, they were brought from the fort. On the way, and very near the spot where Long, Elliot, Williams and others were so cruelly butchered, Satank loosed his heavy iron handcuffs by gnawing and stripping the flesh to the bone. He immediately, and wild cat like, seized a Spencer carbine, and attempted the life of a soldier in the presence of the guard and his fellow prisoners. He was a large, powerful, muscular man, and thus exhibited his extraordinary will power, and preference for death, rather than take the chance of receiving justice in a Texas court. As quick as he was observed, a file of soldiers instantly poured a volley into the desperado and he fell lifeless at their feet. This sudden and unexpected termination of Satank's existence, created the greatest consternation and

Figure 14.1: SATANTA AND BIG TREE WITH THEIR WARRIORS FIRING A WAGON TRAIN IN JACK COUNTY WITH SAMUEL ELLIOTT, A TEAMSTER, CHAINED TO THE WAGON WHEEL.

alarm in Satanta and Big Tree, and the balance of the trip, while they were perfectly docile, they were placed under the closest surveillance until lodged in, and chained to, the floor of their prison cells.

The arrest of Satanta and Big Tree occasioned general rejoicing throughout northwest Texas; and it is not to be wondered at when the condition of the country and the number of atrocious murders are considered. As soon as the prisoners were taken to Jacksboro, and the fact was made known to Judge So ward, of the thirteenth judicial district, at Weatherford, His Honor fixed an immediate trial at the term then ensuing.

THE TRIAL

Commenced on Wednesday, July 5, 1871, Judge Charles Soward on the bench. The district attorney, S. W. T. Lanham, Esq., of Weatherford, conducted the prosecution. Thomas Ball, then of Weatherford, but now of Jacksboro, and J.A. Woolfork, Esq., of Weatherford, appeared for the prisoners. The court room was densely packed, during the progress of the case, with men, women and children. It occasioned the greatest curiosity and excitement. *The Indians were the first and only chiefs ever tried before a civil court in America!* The interest, therefore, as might be supposed, was intense. The prisoners were taken to and from the court room under a military guard, and in the hall of justice the strong arm of military power protected the civil authorities during the trial, conviction and sentence of the murderers. While there was no attempt on the part of the citizens or others to interfere in the administration of justice, it was deemed judicious to have the prisoners strongly guarded so as to prevent the possibility of injury to themselves or to others.

This remarkable cause progressed before Thomas W. Williams (now mayor of Jacksboro and brother of "Blue Jeans" Williams, governor of Indiana), John Cameron, Everett Johnson, H. B. Vernor, S. Cooper, William Hensley, John H. Brown, Peyton Lynn, Peter Hart, Daniel Brown, L. P. Bunch and James Cooley, twelve intelligent and conscientious jurors. The principal witnesses were Colonel R. S. Mackenzie, Lowrie Tatem and Thomas Brazeal. The prisoners were all ably represented by Messrs. Ball and Woolfork, both of whom were faithful to their clients. They took advantage of every legal technicality and conducted their defense with excellent judgment and decided impressiveness. At the conclusion of the testimony, during which the witnesses passed through a searching examination, the counsel for the prisoners talked long and well to the jury. The learned and eloquent district attorney, S. W. T. Lanham, Esq. (of the Weatherford law firm of Watts, Lanham & Roach), then closed with a powerful address, from which we extract as follows:

"This is a novel and important trial, and has, perhaps, no precedent in the history of American criminal jurisprudence. The remarkable character of the prisoners, who are leading representatives of their race; their crude and barbarous appearance; the gravity of the charge; the number of victims; the horrid brutality and inhuman butchery inflicted upon the bodies of the dead; the dreadful and terrific spectacle of seven men, who were husbands, fathers, brothers, sons and lovers, on the morning of the dark and bloody day of this atrocious deed, and rose from their rude tents bright with hope, in the prime and pride of manhood— found, at a later hour, beyond recognition in every condition of horrid disfiguration, unutterable mutilation and death, lying

Stark and stiff
Under the hoofs of vaunting enemies!

"This vast collection of our border people; this sea of faces, including distinguished gentlemen, civic and military, who have come hither to witness the triumph of law and justice over barbarity and assassination; the matron and the maiden, the gray haired sire and the immature lad, who have been attracted to this tribunal by this unusual occasion, all conspire to surround this case with thrilling and extraordinary interest. Though we were to pause in silence, the cause I represent would exclaim with trumpet-tongue:

"Satanta, the veteran council chief of the Kiowas—the orator, the diplomat, the counselor of his tribe—the pulse of his race:—Big Tree, the young war chief, who leads in the thickest of the fight, and follows no one in the chase—the mighty warrior athlete, with the speed of the deer and the eye of the eagle, are before this bar, in the charge of the law!' So they would be described by Indian admirers, who live in more secure and favored lands, remote from the frontier—'where distance lends enchantment' to the imagination—where the story of Pocahontas and the speech of Logan, the Mingo, are read, and the dread sound of the war whoop is not heard. We who see them to-day, disrobed of all their fancied graces, exposed in the light of reality, behold them through far different lenses .' We recognize in Satanta the arch fiend of treachery and blood— the cunning Cataline—the promoter of strife—the breaker of treaties signed by his own hand—the inciter of his fellows to rapine and murder—the artful dealer in bravado while in the powwow, and the most abject coward in the field, as well as the most canting and double-tongued hypocrite when detected and overcome! In Big Tree we perceive the tiger-demon, who has tasted blood and loves it as his food—who stops at no crime, how black soever—who is swift at every species of ferocity, and pities not at any sight of agony or death—he can scalp, burn, torture, mangle and deface his victims with all the superlatives of cruelty, and have no feeling of sympathy or remorse. They are both hideous and loathsome in appearance, and we look in vain to see in them anything to be admired, or even endured. Still, these rough 'sons of the wood' have been commiserated; the measures of the poet and the pen of romance have been invoked to grace the 'melancholy history' of the red man. Powerful legislative influences have been brought to bear to procure for them annuities, reservations and supplies. Federal munificence has fostered and nourished them, fed and clothed them; from their strongholds of protection they have come down upon us 'like wolves on the fold;' treaties have been solemnly made with them, wherein they have been considered with all the formalities of quasi nationalities; immense financial 'rings' have had their origin in and drawn their vitality from the Indian question;' unblushing corruption has stalked abroad, created and kept alive through

'— the poor Indian, whose untutored mind
Sees God in clouds, or hears Him in the wind.'

"Mistaken sympathy for these vile creatures has kindled the flames around the cabin of the pioneer and despoiled him of his hard earnings, murdered and scalped our people, and carried off our women into captivity worse than death. For many years, predatory and numerous bands of these 'pets of the government' have waged the most relentless and heartrending warfare upon our frontier, stealing our property and killing our citizens. We have cried aloud for help; as segments of the grand aggregate of the country we have begged for relief; deaf ears have been turned to our cries, and the story of our wrongs has been discredited. Had it not been for General W. T. Sherman and his most opportune journey through this section—his personal observation of the debris of this scene of slaughter, the ensanguined corpses of the murdered teamsters, and the entire evidences of this dire tragedy, it may well be doubted whether these brutes in human shape, would ever have been brought to trial; for it is a fact, well known in Texas, that stolen property has been traced to the very doors of the. reservation, and there identified by our people, to no purpose. We are greatly indebted to the military arm of the government for kindly offices and co-operation in procuring the arrest and transference of the defendants. If the entire management of the Indian question were submitted to that gallant and distinguished army officer (General Mackenzie) who graces this occasion with his dignified presence, our frontier would soon enjoy immunity from these marauders.

"It speaks well for the humanity of our laws and the tolerance of this people, that the prisoners are permitted to be tried in this Christian land, and by this Christian tribunal. The learned court has, in all things, required the observance of the same rules of procedure—the same principles of evidence—the same judicial methods, from the presentment of the indictment down to the charge soon to be given by his honor, that are enforced in the trial of a white man. You, gentlemen of the jury, have sworn that you can and will render a fair and impartial verdict. Were we to practice lex talionis, no right of trial by jury would be allowed these monsters; on the contrary, as they have treated their victims, so it would be measured unto them.

"The definition of murder is so familiar to the court, and has been so frequently discussed before the country, that any technical or elaborate investigation of the subject, under the facts of this case, would seem unnecessary. Under our statute, 'all murder committed in the perpetration, or in the attempt at the perpetration of robbery is murder in the first degree.' Under the facts of the case we might well rest upon this clause of the statute in the determination of the grade of the offense. The testimony discloses these salient features: About the time indicated by the charge, the defendants, with other chiefs, and a band of more than fifty warriors, were absent from their reservation at Fort Sill; they were away about thirty days—a sufficient length of time to make this incursion and return; that upon their return they brought back their booty—the forty mules, guns and pistols, and camp supplies of the deceased; that Satanta made a speech in presence of the interpreter, Lowrie Tatem, the Indian agent at Fort Sill, and General Sherman, in which he boasted of having been down to Texas and had a big fight—killing seven Tehannas (Texans) and capturing forty mules, guns, pistols, ammunition, sugar and coffee and other supplies of the train; that he said if any other chief claimed the credit of the victory that he was a liar; that he, Satanta, with Big Tree and Satank (who were present and acquiesced in the statement), were entitled to all the glory.' Here we have his own admission, voluntarily and arrogantly made, describing minutely this whole tragic affair. Then we have the evidence of one of the surviving teamster who tells of the attack upon him and his comrades, by a band of over fifty Indians—of the killing of seven of his comrades and the escape of four others, with himself. Then we have the testimony of the orderly sergeant, who, himself, is an old Indian fighter, and familiar with the modes of attack and general conduct of the savages. He, with a detachment of soldiers, went out from Fort Richardson to the scene of blood, to bury the dead. He describes how they were scalped, mutilated with tomahawks, shot with arrows; how the wagon master was chained to the wheel and burned, evidently while living; of the revolting and horrible manner in which the dead bodies were mangled and disfigured, and how everything betokened the work and presence of Indians. He further describes the arrows as those of the Kiowas. We learn from him the interesting fact that Indian tribes are known by the peculiar manner in which their arrows are made, like civilized nations are recognized by their flags.

"The same amount and character of testimony were sufficient to convict any white men. 'By their own words let them be condemned.' Their conviction and punishment cannot repair the loss, nor avenge the blood of the good men they have slain; still, it is due to law, justice and humanity that they should receive the highest punishment. This is even too mild and humane for them. Pillage and bloodthirstiness were the motors of this diabolical deed—fondness for torture and intoxication of delight at human agony impelled its perpetration. All the elements of murder in the first degree are found in the case. The jurisdiction of the court is complete, and the State of Texas expects from you a verdict and judgment in accordance with the law and the evidence."

*   *   *   *   *   *   *

We regret our inability to reproduce all the speech of District Attorney Lanham. His pictures of the massacre, the sufferings of the victims, the piercing shrieks of the dying teamsters; his delineation of the habits and miserable, wicked existence of the Kiowas and other tribes, led on by such daring savages as Satanta, Big Tree, Satank and others, and his representations of the scenes and incidents surrounding the numerous Indian raids in Texas, with their scalping processes, their destruction of life and property, combined to make up an appeal to the court and jury, such has rarely been listened to in any court of justice.

SPEECH OF SATANTA

As interpreted by Mr. Jones. It was spoken in the Comanche tongue, that being the dominant vernacular among the Indians of the plains. The Kiowa chief was handcuffed at the time of his speech, which was delivered semi-signal, semi oral, so to speak. Of course the speech can not now be literally reproduced. It is given below as substantially remembered:

"I can not speak with these things upon my wrists [holding up his arms to show the iron bracelets], I am a squaw. Has any thing been heard from the great father? I have never been so near the Tehannas (Texans) before. I look around me and see your braves, squaws and papooses, and I have said in my heart, if I ever get back to my people I will never make war upon you. I have always been the friend of the white man ever since I was so high [indicating by sign the height of a boy]. My tribe have taunted me and called me a squaw because I have been the friend of the Tehannas. I am suffering now for the crimes of bad Indians—of Satank and Lone Wolf and Kicking Bird and Big Bow and Fast Bear and Eagle Heart, and if you will let me go I will kill the three latter with my own hand. I did not kill the Tehannas. I came down Pease river as a big medicine man to doctor the wounds of the braves. I am a big chief among my people, and have great influence among the warriors of my tribe—they know my voice and will hear my word. If you will let me go back to my people, I will withdraw my warriors from

Tehanna. I will take them all across the Red river, and that shall be the line between us and the pale faces. I will wash out the spots of blood and make it a white land and there shall be peace, and the Tehannas may plow and drive their oxen to the banks of the river, but if you kill me it will be like a spark in the prairie—make big fire! burn heap!"

Judge Soward's charge to the jury was delivered Friday, July 8. We are told it was in strict accordance with the horrible facts of the case, as minutely detailed by the witnesses and the law. Every effort was made to obtain a copy of the charge, but without success. W. H. Mitchell, clerk of the district court of Jack county, wrote, May 4, 1877, that the papers in the Satanta case have been a lost and can not be found."

THE VERDICT

The jury was absent but a little while. When they returned and rendered their verdict of "guilty of murder in the first degree," fixing their punishment at death, there was a silence, an indescribable feeling of awe for an instant, when the entire audience broke forth in one shout of rejoicing. The result closed a trial second in importance and interest to none in America.

It gave instantaneous relief to the populace. It seemed as if the thralldom and terrors of the Texas frontiersman were at an end; that business could again resume its Wonted channels; that the community could enjoy a peace unknown to them for years, and that justice had been meted out to two of the most devilish of the worst desperadoes of the age. The prisoners were remanded to the custody of Sheriff Blanchard. Subsequently they were sentenced to be hung on the first day of September, 1871.

On May 29, 1871, Lowrie Tatem, the Fort Sill reservation Indian agent, addressed a letter to General W. T. Sherman, in which he wrote: "Permit me to urge, independent of my conscientious views against capital punishment, as a matter of policy, it would be best for the inhabitants of Texas, that they (meaning Satanta and Big Tree) be not executed for some time, and probably not at all, for the reason that if they are kept as prisoners the Indians will hope to have them released and thus have a restraining influence in their actions. But if they are executed the Indians will be very likely to seek revenge in the wholesale murder of white people."

Indian Agent Tatem also wrote S. W. T. Lanham. Esq., district attorney, June 29, as follows: "In view of the trial of Satanta and Big Tree, Kiowa chiefs, of this agency, permit me to remind thee that two characteristic traits of the Indians are to seek revenge and great dread of imprisonment. From my knowledge of the Indians, I believe if the prisoners should be convicted of murder, it would be a more severe punishment to them to confine them for life than to execute them, and it would probably save the lives of some white people; for if they were executed it is more than probable that some of the other Kiowas would seek revenge in the murder of some white citizens. This is judging the case from a policy standpoint. But if we judge it from a Christian standpoint, I believe we should, in all cases, even of murder in the first degree, confine a person for life, and leave to God his prerogative to determine when a person has lived long enough."

COMMUTATION RECOMMENDED.

WEATHERFORD, PARKER COUNTY, TEXAS,

JULY 10, 1871

Governor E. J. Davis.

Sir—I have the honor to say * * that the last term is regarded of more interest to our frontier than any court that has ever been held in the State. Upon arriving at Jacksboro, we despatched a posse of five citizens to Fort Sill, for the necessary witnesses, and through the assistance of Colonel MacKenzie, commanding United States army at Fort Richardson, General Grierson, commanding at Fort Sill, and Lowrie Tatem, Indian agent, we obtained the necessary witnesses for the State, and after a fair and impartial trial, the defendants having the best counsel at the command of the court, the jury returned a verdict of murder in the first degree, and fixed their punishment at death.

Mr. Tatem expressed a strong desire that they should be punished by imprisonment for life, instead of death, but the jury thought differently. I passed sentence upon them on the eighth of July, and fixed the time of execution at Friday, September 1, next. I must say, here, that I concur with Mr. Tatem as to the punishment; simply, however, upon a politic view of the matter. Mr. Tatem has indicated that if they are tried, convicted and punished by imprisonment, that he would render the civil authorities all the assistance in his power to bring others of those tribes on the reservation who have been guilty of outrages in Texas to trial and just punishment. I would have petitioned your excellency to commute their punishment to imprisonment for life, were it not that I know a great majority of the people on the frontier demand their execution. Your excellency, however, acting for the weal of the State at large, and free from the passions of the masses, may see fit to commute their punishment. If so, I say amen! Now, while entertaining the opinion that the present policy of the United States toward these wild tribes, is founded on supreme folly, nevertheless, I see in this new phase of the Quaker policy (which has culminated in the trial and conviction of the great chief, Satanta and brave Big Tree, by civil authority) a solution of our difficulties; and, if we only use our vantage ground, I think we will be speedily redeemed from the ravages of all the reserve Indians on our borders.

During the trial of Satanta and Big Tree, it appeared from legitimate testimony that Big Bow, Fast Bear, and Eagle Heart, were in the last raid that resulted in the murder of seven men and the capture of forty-one head of fine mules. Now, I most earnestly request your excellency to issue your requisition for the above named Indians, to be turned over to the sheriff of Jack county. You will please send your commission through General Reynolds, to Colonel MacKenzie at Fort Richardson. Colonel MacKenzie informed me that he is ready and will execute the commission, and Tatem, the agent, is under promise to render all the assistance in his power.

With many wishes for your good health, I remain with much respect. Your very obedient servant,

Charles Soward,
Judge Thirteenth Judicial District, Texas.

Governor's Office,
Austin, August 2, 1871.

Dear Sir—Your communication of the tenth ult. has been received recommending the commutation of sentence in the case of Satanta and Big Tree. I have thought your recommendation a good one, and have accordingly directed that the sentence of these two Indians be commuted to imprisonment for life.

Respectfully,

Edm'd J. Davis, *Gover-*
nor.

To Charles Soward, Judge of Thirteenth District, Weatherford, Parker Co., Texas.

COMMUTATION OF SENTENCE.

Governor Davis, on August 2, 1871, issued the following proclamation commuting the sentences of Satanta and Big Tree to imprisonment for life:

The State of Texas,

> *To all to whom these Presents shall come:*

Whereas, At the July term, A. D. 1871, of the District Court of Jack county, in said State, one Satanta and Big Tree, known as Indians of the Kiowa tribe, were tried and convicted on a charge of murder, and sentenced therefor to suffer the penalty of death on the first day of September, A. D. 1871; and, *whereas,* it is deemed that a commutation of said sentence to imprisonment for life will be more likely to operate as a restraint upon others of the tribe to which these Indians belong; and, *whereas,* the killing for which these Indians were sentenced can hardly be considered as a just consideration of the animus as coming within the technical crime of murder under the statutes of the State, but rather as an act of savage warfare; *now, therefore,* I, Edmund J. Davis, Governor of Texas, by virtue of the authority vested in me by the constitution and laws of this State, do hereby commute the sentence of Satanta and Big Tree to imprisonment for life, at hard labor, in the State penitentiary, and hereby direct the clerk of the District

Court of Jack County to make this commutation of sentence a matter of record in his office.

REMOVAL TO THE PENITENTIARY.

Headquarters Dep't of Texas and Louisiana,
San Antonio, Texas, September 12, 1871.
[Special Order No. 185.]

IV. The Governor of the State of Texas, by his proclamation, dated August 2, having commuted the sentence of death of Satanta and Big Tree, Kiowa Indian chiefs, to imprisonment for life, at hard labor, in the State Penitentiary, and having requested the commander of this military department to cause said Indian chiefs to be delivered to the warden, of said penitentiary; therefore, the commanding officer at Fort Richardson, Texas, will send, under suitable guard, the prisoners Satanta and Big Tree to Huntsville, Texas, and cause them to be delivered to the warden of the said penitentiary. Receipt for said prisoners will be taken from the warden, and the original forwarded to department headquarters. The commissioned officer in charge of the guard will be held directly responsible for the sure custody and entire personal safety of the prisoners *en route* and until formally delivered to the warden, and to this end all communication of the prisoners by civilians will be carefully prevented and strictly forbidden.

By command of Major J. J. Reynolds.

H. Clay Wood, *Ass't Adj't General.*

The sentence of the murderous chiefs had scarcely been pronounced (July 8, 1871) before Enoch Hoag, Superintendent of Indian Affairs, Lawrence, Kansas, was beseeching the President of the United States (July 19, 1871) for executive clemency. He gave as his reasons for asking that the death sentence be commuted to *imprisonment for life,* that if these chiefs were hung, he feard the consequences to the border inhabitants of Texas, as resulting from the executions. As the result of this intercession Governor Davis, under influences brought to bear upon him by the United States Government, on August 2, 1871, commuted the sentences to imprisonment for life. What other influences or motives prompted President Grant to interpose further in behalf of these murderous chiefs, we have not been able to learn, but it is a fact that Governor Davis set them at liberty upon the recommendation of the President, as the following from the records of the penitentiary will show: "Set at liberty by Governor Davis, August 19, 1873, upon recommendation of the President of the United States upon parole." Satanta and Big Tree were accordingly set at liberty upon that day, and escorted from Huntsville back to the reservation. How well these murderous villains observed the "parole," without going into details, can be seen from the following extract from Lieutenant General Sheridan's order of October 30, 1874, written from the headquarters of the military division of the Missouri, in camp at Sheridan Roost, on the North Canadian river, directing Captain C. H. Carlton, commanding at Fort Sill, to return Satanta to prison. The extract is as follows: "That as the Kiowa Chief Satanta, now in the guard house, at Fort Sill, has violated the conditions on which he was released from the State penitentiary in Texas, that you return him in charge of a commissioned officer and suitable guard, to that institution. His Excellency, the Governor of Texas, will give the necessary instructions for his re-incarceration." Satanta was accordingly returned to the penitentiary November 8, 1874. Big Tree has never been captured, although he, too, has flagrantly violated his parole on several occasions. Big Bow is in the penitentiary as a hostage.

Previous to his parole, Satanta did very little work, sometimes picking wool and pulling shucks for mattresses, only working when inclined to do so. After he was returned to prison the second time, he did very little, with the exception of making bows and arrows. Big Tree, before being paroled, worked constantly bottoming chairs, and became very expert, and could put in as many or more bottoms than any other hand.

[Note.—Since the publication of the book from which the above data was taken, we find from the report of Adjutant General King, September, 1884, that Satanta either committed suicide or broke his neck in attempting to escape from the penitentiary. The precise facts, the Attorney General did not have.]

The Indians were continually raiding in Young, Jack, Parker, Palo Pinto, and in fact, throughout all the northwestern counties, and both life and property of the citizens were almost at the complete mercy of these bloodthirsty demons. Their depredations became so frequent, and their outrages so numerous that the Fourteenth Legislature of Texas authorized the raising of a battalion, and as will be seen in the succeeding article, Major Jones became commander.

Chapter 15

Major John B. Jones

THE Fourteenth Legislature of Texas, which convened in January, 1874, passed an act authorizing a battalion of rangers to be raised for the frontier service, and Major John B. Jones, of Corsicana, was appointed by Governor Coke, to the command.

We will briefly give an outline of the services performed by Major Jones and his battalion of rangers, taken from his report to General William Steele, Adjutant General of the State.

(The first of September, 1875, the battalion consisted of five companies, of thirty-three men each.)

"During the first six months of the service there were more than forty parties of Indians on the frontier, being about the average, so the settlers say, of what it had been for several years past. We had fourteen engagements with them. During the second six months we had four engagements. On the first of May, 1875, there were eight parties of Indians in at one time. I caught one of these parties and killed five. Since May last only six bands of Indians have visited us, and I have had only one fight. Have had in all, nineteen engagements with Indians, in one of which we killed all but three, and in another two.

"We have killed twenty-seven Indians that we know of and ten or twelve more we have reason to believe have been killed. My losses have been two men killed and six wounded. On the twelfth of July, with two officers and thirty-four men, I met a large war party of well armed and well mounted Comanches, Kiowas and Apaches, numbering between one hundred and twenty-five and one hundred and fifty, commanded, as I have since learned, by the celebrated Kiowa chief Lone Wolf, and in an engagement of several hours duration defeated them and forced them to retreat. My loss was D. W. C. Bailey and W. A. Glass killed, company B, and Lee Conn and George Moore wounded. Twelve horses killed and two wounded. Three Indians were killed and three wounded. This fight took place in Lost Valley, Young county."

In his reports, Major Jones says: "About September 15, Lieutenant Telesfero Montes, of El Paso county, frontiersman, with twelve men of his command, attacked a party of seven Indians, killed two and captured five horses."

"On the eighteenth of November Lieutenant B. F. Best, company E, frontier battalion, with sixteen men, overtook a party of Indians near Brownwood, Brown county, after following them from Coleman county, a distance of twenty miles. Three Indians were killed, one wounded and most of their camp equipage captured. Two men of company E were slightly wounded and one horse killed.

"On November 21, 1874, Lieutenant D. W. Roberts, company D, frontier battalion, and a detachment of his company, pursued and engaged in Menard county a party of eleven Indians (Comanches), killing five on the field and capturing three horses, guns, pistols, etc. As his horses were too much fatigued to pursue the remaining five Indians the chase was continued by Lieutenant L. P. Beavert and his men, who succeeded in killing another Indian and wounding one. The loss on our side in these fights was the wounding of three horses."

It is plainly evident from the foregoing that the gallant Major did all that could be done for the protection of an extensive frontier with the small force at his command. Besides fighting and chasing Indians, much of the time was occupied in quieting bloody feuds among the border settlements, where the civil authorities were powerless to act, and capturing numerous lawless desperadoes by whom at that time the frontiers were greatly infested. He also recaptured from the Indians in the various encounters he had with them a large number of stolen horses and other property which were restored to the proper owners. There is no doubt that but for the protection given by Major Jones and his little battalion the settlement of many frontier counties would have been greatly retarded, and many defenseless families murdered by the savages.

Major John B. Jones was born in Fairfield District, South Carolina, December 22, 1834, and with his father, Colonel Henry Jones, came to Texas in 1838, and settled in Travis county. Thus it will be seen he was only four years of age when he landed in Texas. During the war between the States, he was among the first to enlist in the service of the Confederacy. Although he entered as a private, he did not long remain so, as shortly afterwards he received the appointment of adjutant of the Fifteenth Texas Infantry, which served in the trans-Mississippi department till the close of the war. Recognizing his gallantry and capacity for command, Generals Harrison, Green, Smith, Polignac and Taylor, recommended him for promotion to the rank of major in his old regiment, the line officers waiving their claims in his favor (something unusual). The appointment was made, but owing to the irregularities of the mail his commission did not reach him until after the war had closed.

Without solicitation on his part, he was appointed, as before stated, by Governor Coke, major of the frontier battalion of State troops. We are sorry we are not in possession of the particulars of the various engagements in which Major Jones participated while in command of the troops stationed on the borders. We have only had his reports made to the Adjutant General, to go by, which merely give the general results, and this is our explanation of the very meagre accounts herein contained. One of the Texas journals of that day, in speaking of Major Jones, said: "As an Indian fighter, Major Jones has acquired a reputation unsurpassed, and now that a quietus has been put upon the red man, he is devoting special attention to the rest of the outlaws and lawless characters generally among more civilized classes. In this field he has so far achieved a success no less conspicuous than on the frontier."

While in command of the frontier troops, Major Jones became perfectly familiar with the condition of affairs, which required the strong arm of the government to protect both the citizen and his property, and Governor Roberts, after his election to the gubernatorial chair, recognizing the peculiar fitness of the man, appointed him Adjutant General of the State, which position he filled up to the time of his death, at his home in Austin, July 19, 1881. He was a man suited for private or public—for civil or military life. He possessed the unpretentious, but dignified mien of a chivalrous southern gentleman, and was always armed with the "courage of his convictions." His word was a bond of honor, ever to be respected and never violated. His engagements were sacred and inviolable. He was a man in whom his fellow man had implicit confidence. In short, he was "an honest man—the noblest work of God." In these degenerate days, when honesty seems to be considered a commodity of traffic, it is refreshing to contemplate the character of one upon whose escutcheon rests not even the taint of suspicion. He was a courtly knight, clothed in the panoply of a Christian gentleman.

Chapter 16

Heroic Defense of the Dillard Brothers

1869

WE are indebted to Colonel E. S. Graham for the following account of the heroic defense of two beardless youths (Henry and Willie Dillard) against thirty Comanche warriors.

Early in the autumn of 1869, I arrived in Texas, from Louisville, Kentucky, accompanied by two young men, Dillard and Dorrell, who wished to see Texas, and the "wild west" generally. Late in the following spring

I returned to Kentucky, leaving these young men in Texas to improve a place yet known as Fort Davis, on the Clear fork of the Brazos, about eight miles below Fort Griffin. In 1872, Dillard planted an abandoned farm, mostly in water melons, on the west side of the Brazos, about four miles above Belknap, in Young county. He had written to me previously that he was very anxious to have his brother Willie with him (a lad about eleven years old) who was then in Kentucky. I therefore furnished Willie with tickets to Fort Worth, and gave such directions as would enable him to reach that place, and from thence to Fort Griffin via Belknap. He arrived safely at Henry's lonely abode, and shortly afterwards they went to Fort Griffin with a two horse wagon loaded with watermelons, which they disposed of at from fifty cents to one dollar and fifty cents each. On their way home, and when about sixteen miles from Fort Griffin, Henry was aroused from a slumber into which he had fallen by Willie exclaiming "Brother Henry, the Indians have got us." Henry quickly looked up and discovered about thirty mounted Indians ahead of them in the road, painted and in full war costume. He instantly seized his repeating rifle, jumped from the wagon and told Willie to follow him. After running a short distance, Henry halted, and turning, fired upon the foremost Indians, but without any effect except to check temporarily their approach. Taking advantage of this, the boys ran on in the direction of some timber upon a creek until they were compelled to halt again and confront their pursuers. Again Henry fired his rifle, and as before, without any effect except to retard their advance for a moment. But just as he was in the act of firing the third time (as he has told me subsequently) the advice I had frequently given to Dorell and himself in our travels came to mind. "In a fight with mounted Indians always aim low, as in doing so they are unable to ward off the shot with their shields, at which they are exceedingly expert, and you will be sure to hit either the rider or his horse—and a dismounted warrior is already half whipped." Following my advice he aimed low the third time, and at the report of the rifle, both the horse and the rider fell to the ground. Seeing their comrade fall, the Indians gave a terrible yell and rushed upon the boys. Soon Willie's piercing shriek, "Oh! brother Henry," caused him to turn round, and he discovered an Indian warrior just in the act of lifting Willie upon his horse. Raising his gun quickly he fired and dropped him dead from his horse. This again checked the Indians momentarily, and the boys once more made for the timber as fast as they could go. But when about twenty paces from the point of timber they were endeavoring to reach, Henry stumbled and fell, but quickly regaining his feet, he turned and shot one of the foremost warriors, who with scalping knife in hand, was in the act of dismounting, thinking no doubt that he was killed or wounded. In another moment the boys reached the timber and this unequal contest came to an end, for the Indians had been so roughly handled, they dared not follow them further. The boys came out of it without a scratch. This band of Indians, on their return to Fort Sill, reported that they had had a fight with a "heap d—d big captain and his little boy," and that their "medicine" was too strong for them. When night came the brothers went to the nearest ranch. There they obtained horses, proceeded to Fort Griffin; and reported the facts to the officer in command, who at once sent a detachment of dragoons in pursuit of the Indians. They discovered that the band had divided into two parties—one of which had carried off the dead and wounded. Following the trail of this party in a day or so they came to a fresh camp, in which they found several beds of grass covered with clots of blood. On a mound near by, the bodies of three "good Ingens" were found. Other bodies were subsequently found, and on his return the officer in command of this detachment of dragoons, asserted that he was satisfied that Henry Dillard and his little brother Willie had killed and wounded eleven Indians in the fight, besides five horses left dead on the ground.

Chapter 17

Brit Johnson, A Negro—His Thrilling Career

1864

TO COLONEL GRAHAM we are also indebted for the following thrilling narrative. [This is the same Brit Johnson incidentally referred to in the article contributed by Captain Barry, published elsewhere in this book.] The free air of the prairies, the stern trials of frontier life, have always developed a manly, self-reliant and courageous people in Texas. During the war between the States there lived in Young county on Peters' Colony, survey number seven hundred and two, situated on the south side of Elm creek, about three miles from its junction with the Brazos river, Moses Johnson, grandfather of Parker Johnson. With Moses Johnson, lived Britton Johnson (commonly known as Brit), a shining jet black negro of splendid physique and fine expression of face, which plainly manifested his kindly and manly characteristics. Brit had a wife and four children, all of whom he dearly loved. His master, Moses Johnson, had allowed him the enlarged liberty which belongs to the frontier, often relying in part upon his strong arm to help defend the family and neighborhood from the raids of hostile bands of Indians. On the thirteenth day of October, 1864, while Brit Johnson was absent in Parker county after supplies for his master's family, one thousand Comanche warriors swept through the doomed little neighborhood carrying death and desolation to every hearth stone. They killed Brit's son Jim, Joel Meyers, Doctor T. J. Wilson, James McCoy and his son Miles, the widow Durgan and five out of fifteen Texan rangers, and wounded many others. They carried away as captives the widow Patrick, her two grand daughters, daughters of the slain widow Durgan, and the negro's wife and those of his children whom they had not murdered. They also started with Joe, son of the slain widow Durgan, but being sick and unable to stand the fatigue of the march, they killed him on the second day's journey. When the negro reached home, he shared in and felt the common ruin to the community, but was not paralyzed by his great grief, and with a courage possessed by few he determined to have back his wife and children or perish in the effort. Under the generous treatment of his master he became the owner of a large number of horses and cattle, and when peace, like an angel of mercy, with healing on her wings, blessed the country and gave him his freedom, he tried every pathway to recover his lost ones. He visited the forts in the Indian Territory, and offered for ransom all he had. He made inquiries of Indian agents, and of Indians who visited the agencies, but all in vain. Finally he returned to his Texas home cast down and disappointed by his futile efforts, but not unnerved. He determined to go alone hundreds of miles through a howling wilderness, infested with hostile savages and find the Indians who held his wife as a slave. It was useless to ask any one to go with him on such a perilous mission, so he carefully packed with provisions one horse, and mounting his favorite black steed, he started from Young county to seek the villages of the wild tribes far out on the plains. He traveled for several weeks continuously, mostly by night, in a northwesterly direction, through what is known as the Panhandle of Texas.

One evening when about thirty miles distant from the Indian encampment, where his wife and children were, he discovered upon a mountain peak the Indian pickets. They discovered him about the same time. Brit signaled them as a friend, approached them, and informed them as best he could that his purposes were friendly, that he wanted to find his wife and be one of the tribe. These pickets detained him for three days—probably awaiting instructions from the chief of the village—when he was escorted into the main Indian encampment. Here he was kindly received; did everything in his power to disarm the suspicion of the Indians; was given his wife and children and became a member of the tribe. It was the custom of the Indians when hunting for game to scatter out over the plains in small squads to kill and cure their meat. The negro took advantage of this custom, *got* his wife and children and one of the captured Miss Durgan's in his hunting party, and on a seasonable occasion, in the summer of 1865, under the friendly shades of night, set out with his party on horseback for his Texas home, which he finally reached in safety, guided only by the stars and his general knowledge of the country. His stay among the wild tribes of the plains gave him a fund of information as to their manner and mode of fighting, the meaning of their telegraph smoke signals, etc., and after his return home it was Brit's greatest delight to talk over with his old friends his life spent among the Indians, and relate his adventures, privations and hardships, incident to his hazardous mission. It was not destined, however, that Brit should enjoy for a long season the inestimable happiness which the reclamation of his loved ones brought him. The Indians never forgot or forgave what they deemed his treachery to their tribe. In the latter part of January, 1871, while returning from Weatherford with a couple of colored men, who were to assist him in gathering in his stock, they camped over night on the old military road, about four miles east of Salt creek. Unaware to each other a freight train was camped on the same road about one mile and a half further west. Early the next morning, between day light and sun up, while the freighters were rounding in their stock, about twenty-five mounted warriors suddenly appeared and began hostile maneuvers, but about this time rapid and continued firing began at Brit's camp, to which this party of warriors hastened. The freighters, taking refuge on a brush mound, from whence they could see, witnessed the fight at Brit's camp. A large band of painted warriors, once the friends, but now the deadly enemies of Brit, had surrounded him and his two companions, and were making the very earth tremble beneath the clattering hoofs of their horses, while their hideous yells broke the stillness of the early morning. Brit's two companions fell early in the action, but his courage was equal to the occasion, and the determined negro, who knew his time had come, resolved to sell his life dearly to his foes. Like the great king making Baron on his last bloody field, the negro drew his bowie knife and deliberately cut the throat of his favorite black steed that had borne him safely through many perils, and of his body made a breastwork. Armed with his own weapon and that of his fallen comrades, Brit fought with a desperation almost supernatural, killing and wounding many of his assailants before he went to eternal rest. When the battle ground was afterward visited, one hundred and seventy-three cartridge shells were counted lying around his dead body. The savage demons cut off his ears, one of his arms, disemboweled him, then killed and thrust in his pet little dog, besides otherwise fearfully mutilating his person, but his dauntless spirit had taken its flight before one of them was able to lay his bloody hands upon him. The remains of Brit and his two companions lie buried on the north side of the road, near the spot where they fell.

Chapter 18

Captain Curiton's Fight on Wolf Creek

1860

THE year 1860 was fraught with many thrilling incidents in Texas. The Indians in that year visited almost every portion of the frontier, and many lives were lost and a vast amount of property was stolen. Several companies were stationed along the frontier border for the protection of the settlers. The command of one of these companies was given to Captain Jack Curiton. As soon as the necessary preparations were made, Captain Jack, with his company, started out in search of the enemy. In a few days he came across an Indian trail leading northwest. This they followed beyond the Double Mountain fork of the Brazos and out into the Staked Plains. They continued on in these dreary plains for two days, when they were compelled to abandon the trail for want of water. Their stock of provisions was exhausted, and game was also very scarce in those desolate regions. They therefore turned their course southward, intending to strike the Colorado river or some one of its tributaries. In the meantime they succeeded in finding a

little bad water every day, but for five days they had nothing
to eat. Finally their hunters killed a fine, fat bear and several
deer, and this timely supply relieved their pressing wants, and
from thence on they found an abundance of good water and
grass. Late in the evening one day they came to an Indian trail
leading pretty much in the direction they were traveling. The
trail seemed to be several days old, but they followed it until
dark and then encamped. The next morning they took the trail
again, and about ten o'clock the spies, who had been sent in
advance, rode to the top of a small mountain, and from its
summit they discovered some objects in the distance, but were
unable to tell what they were. They hurried on to find out what
it was they had seen, and soon discovered that it was a party
of Indians going towards the Colorado settlements. The spies
hastened back to the company and told Captain Curiton they
had seen the Indians. The company pushed ahead on the trail
as rapidly as possible, and about four o'clock in the evening
they discovered the Indians on foot, engaged in shooting prairie
dogs with their bows and arrows. The Indians had their camp
in the bottom on Wolf creek, and were out killing prairie dogs
for their supper.

The Texans and the Indians discovered each other about the
same time, and the Indians at once began to retreat. Captain
Curiton, knowing there was no time to be lost, ordered his
men to charge them. The order was promptly obeyed, and the
Indians being hard pressed by the Texans fled into the bottom;
but before they could reach it, the Texans poured a deadly fire
upon them, killing several and wounding others. Panic stricken,
the rest leaped into the creek and concealed themselves among
the drift and thickets along the banks. The Texans then began
to search for those who had secreted themselves. One had
hidden himself under a willow bush, near a large pile of drift.

James Lane approached the bush where the Indian was hidden, and stooped down to look under it. At that instant the Indian shot an arrow at him, which passed through his abdomen and lodged in the back bone, and a second arrow went through his hand.

When the fight was over, the Texans went to the Indian camp, and took all their camp equipage, consisting of blankets, buffalo robes, one rifle, nine horses and mules and ten saddles. Only one Indian made his escape, which he did by mounting a pony, bare back. The Texans made a litter on which they carried Mr. Lane to Fort Chadborne. He lived but a few days.

Chapter 19

Indian Warfare on the North-western Border.

1857

WE are indebted to Captain R. B. Barry, of Bosque county, for the following interesting items:

According to promise, I herewith contribute to your historical compilation a short account of such conflicts with the Indians as have occurred in my own vicinity, and within my own knowledge.

I will commence my narrative with the winter of 1857, for it was in that year that the first blood of my neighbors was shed in their conflicts with Indians. On one occasion, Mr. Renfrew and his son were out horse hunting on the head of Meridian creek, and whilst there they were attacked by Indians. Young Renfrew was killed and scalped on the instant. His father was riding a good horse, and rode four miles after receiving his death wound. He fell off dead, and the horse returning home riderless revealed the sad fact to the family that the father and husband was no more.

A party immediately went in search of the missing ones. Young Renfrew's body was found about two weeks after he was killed, but the old man—or rather his mutilated remains – were not found until after the lapse of two years. They were found by a Mr. Rabb. Near by was a saddle which was identified by the family as the one Mr. Renfrew was riding when he left home.

In the latter portion of the same year (1857) Mr. Bean, a relative of the Bean of Texas history, and his negro man, while returning home to the Leon river from some of the older settlements, where he had been to buy corn, was attacked by a party of Indians near the same place where they had killed the Renfrews. From the number of arrow marks and bullet holes in the wagon bed, it was supposed that the Indians had paid dearly for their trophies.

The next day the same party of Indians came in sight of my place and attacked a Mr. Johnson, who was returning from the lower country with breadstuffs, and who was driving two yoke of cattle. He was murdered at the foot of a high peak, which has ever since been known as "Johnson's Peak," They took Mr. Johnson's little boy, a lad eight years of age, a prisoner. They also killed several of the oxen, emptied the meal and flour in the road and carried away the sacks.

Some eight or ten days after this, as Hinson Roberts and party were following an Indian trail, along which a good many of their stolen cattle had been driven, they came across this little boy about forty miles from the nearest house. The little fellow was nearly dead with hunger and cold-the Indians having, as they usually do, stripped him of his clothing. The boy had slipped out of camp one cold night, in the same apparel that nature gave him, and came across some cattle that had ropes attached to them; no doubt some that had escaped from a marauding party of Indians. He was trying to stay among these cattle, supposing that they would protect him from the wolves. The little fellow was taken home, and is still living.

The same party of Indians stole from my settlement about one hundred and thirty head of horses, sixty of them belonging to me.

During this same year the Indians made a good many raids into Bosque county, and also the county of Erath. I will relate one incident that occurred in the winter of 1857. A party of Indians came down by the upper settlements on the North Bosque and killed a part of two families. They took two ladies, Mrs. Woods and Mrs. Lemly, some two miles from the house, and, after using them in the most savage and brutal manner, they murdered and scalped both. They also carried off two young ladies, the Misses Lemly, but turned them loose after two days travel. The next day this same party came across two young men, the Monroes, on Spring creek, seven miles from my ranch, where they were opening a farm, and killed both. The Indians met with no resistance, as they took the young men completely by surprise. They left a one hundred dollar bill lying on the ground near where they murdered the young men, probably knowing nothing of its value.

Late the same evening they killed young Knight on Neil's creek, fifteen miles from the scene of their former murders. The next day they wounded two Baptist ministers near the corner of Bell county. One of them died afterwards from the effects of his wound.

Figure 19.1: JOHNSON'S LITTLE BOY FOLLOWING THE COWS.

These Indians were pursued by the citizens, but owing to their rapid retreat they failed to overtake them.

Whenever such raiding parties of Indians were followed, it was invariably observed that after a time the trail divided, and that a part of the Indians had gone off in the direction of the reservations; and, finding many of our horses on the reservations, we were led to believe that at least a portion of the reserve Indians were concerned in the raids made upon the settlements by the wild tribes.

The feeling of hostility towards the reserve Indians caused by such suspicions was a good deal modified, however, by the soothing story of the interpreter, who told us that we were greatly indebted to these reserve Indians for risking their lives in retaking our stock stolen from us by the wild tribes, and really induced us to believe this, and that they had conferred a favor on us by making us pay ten dollars for every horse returned to us.

However, after Fred Gentry's horse had been found on the upper reserve, in possession of the Comanches, and four of the reserve Indians were killed by Captain Preston and his neighbors, when in the act of driving off a number of stolen horses, we were pretty well satisfied that these reserve Indians were leagued with the wild tribes in raiding on the settlements.

On one occasion Captain Peter Garland, who was following an Indian trail, came near a camp of the lower reservation Indians, and mistaking them for Caddoes, a fight was the consequence, in which — Stephens and — Barnes, two of his men, were killed and ten of the Indians. As this fight took place among the wigwams, some of the squaws and children were killed in the melee.

This was the beginning of the reservation war. The citizens flocked to the protection of those living above, near the reservation; and in a few days there were embodied together seven hundred men, besides some small parties scattered about at different points. Captain Allison Nelson was elected to the command, and it was resolved to make an attack upon the upper reservation, as it was believed our worst enemies were there. Four hundred men were ordered to proceed up the Clear fork of the Brazos, under Colonel John R. Baylor.

While passing up by the lower reservation, Colonel Baylor's men killed and captured some straggling Indians. This brought on a fight with the Indians of the lower reservation. The fight lasted several hours, and was carried on in regular savage style by both parties, each putting to death all the prisoners taken. Many were killed and wounded on both sides. but the Indians having the United States forces under Captain Parmer to fall back upon, there was but one alternative left us--either to draw off or attack Captain Parmer's command.

It is very certain that on this occasion some white men fought against us, but no doubt they were mainly the "dead heads" and hangers on about the reservation, as no United States soldiers were seen in the fight.

During a consultation between Colonels Baylor and Nelson, the Indians of both reservations were thrown together, and, with the United States soldiers protecting them, they left the State of Texas and established their reservation at Fort Cobb, on the upper Wichita, in the Chickasaw nation.

During the most of the time while these events were taking place, I was, with a few well mounted men, reconnoitering the Comanche agency.

As the State Convention that passed the ordinance of secession saw proper to place troops on our frontier after the Federal forces had retired, they ordered Colonel Henry E. McCulloch to proceed at once to the front and take charge of the fort, then occupied by United States soldiers. A portion of my company was at that time encamped on the head of Hubbard's creek, and was ordered out by Governor Houston while I was absent on a scout. Subsequently they were transferred to the Confederate service. When I returned, I found myself in command of a company in the First Texas cavalry, under Colonel Henry E. McCulloch.

Our regiment was stationed in detachments from Red river to the Rio Grande, each about a day's ride apart along the uppermost settlements. The officers were strict in their discipline and drill, with the expectation of soon being ordered to a more glorious field than operating against savages, where every man usually was his own commander. Major Edward Burleson and myself both considered that the time wasted in disciplining and drilling troops for service against Indians was costing the frontier people much blood as well as property, and for this or some other reason Burleson resigned his commission as major.

The first scout of any importance was ordered by Major Burleson, who directed me to meet him at a certain big spring on Red river, nearly a day's ride above the Wichita mountain. The night before the morning on which I was to start an express came in, stating that ten of my men whom I had sent to escort some wagons from Camp Cooper, on the Brazos, to Gooch's ranch, on Red river, had been badly used up by the Indians between the Red Fork of the Brazos and Little Wichita, forty-five miles from Camp Cooper, where I was then stationed.

I sent off one-half of my company that night to their relief and all that could be spared from the post the next morning. They met the remnant of the little detachment at the Red

Fork. After burying young McKay, one of the wounded who had died, and giving such medical aid as we could to the other wounded, we sent them back with an escort. We then proceeded on our way and had been traveling but half a day when we came up with the same Indians that had attacked the wagon escort. But before mentioning the result I will here relate the incidents which took place in the fight between these Indians and the detachment escorting the wagons. The detachment was under the command of Sergeant Erhenback. Eight of the ten men composing it were mortally or seriously wounded, the slightest wound having been received by Sergeant Erhenback, the bullet passing through his stirrup before it struck him. His horse was badly wounded. Eight of their ten horses were killed or wounded. The sergeant reported Corporal Miller as having acted mutinously. Corporal Miller said that during the hottest part of the contest, while surrounded on all sides in the open prairie and Indians cross firing at them from every direction, he (Sergeant Erhenback) had ordered a retreat, to what he thought a better position. Corporal Miller persuaded the boys to fight it out where they were, as they had several dead horses for shelter, and he called the sergeant a coward, whereupon they attempted to shoot each other, but were prevented from doing so by the others.

The fight lasted until the Indians had used up all their ammunition (so they supposed) and fell back. It began at nine a.m. and continued until three p.m., and extended over five miles of open prairie. The wounded men rode such horses as were able to travel, whilst the rest fought around them on foot against four times their number. We learned from some of the reservation Indians that their wild friends lost eight of their warriors in this fight.

We will now relate what occurred after we came up with these Indians two days subsequent to the fight just described. Their force had been increased to about one hundred warriors, and they were making their way toward the settlements. Willie Biffle, who was a long way from the command on the right flank, came in and reported Indian signs. I halted the command and sent twelve men back after the pack mules that had stampeded, They had scarcely gone out of sight over the divide when we heard firing. We hurried to their relief, but not in time to save three of the twelve men from being killed and others wounded. A general fight then ensued. After a short time the Indians began to fall back, notwithstanding they had three to our one.

The fight extended over some ten or twelve miles of ground across the divide, and between the Little Wichita and the Red Fork of the Brazos. Whenever we became somewhat scattered in the chase the Indians would turn and check our advance for a while. They were well armed and equipped and wore a great many savage ornaments. The one the chief wore was composed of feathers, stripped from the quills and tied to his hair, as long as there was a place to tie one, which increased the size of his head until it looked like a large wash tub. He was quite a brave man, but we made his hair and feathers both fly. Many bullets were thrown from their course by his shield, and many were embedded in it. A chance shot from the gun of John L. Hardigree eventually just missed the top of his shield and struck his head, but did not inflict a wound sufficient to kill him. As soon as they perceived that their chief was wounded his warriors rallied around him and moved him away.

Many of our men who were on slow horses had fallen behind, but coming up just then with loaded guns they soon set the Indians traveling again.

We lost three killed in this fight, to wit, Thomas J. Weathersby, Lip Conley and Bud Lane. Two men were wounded. We only killed seven of the Indians that we know of. The next morning our horses were so stiff that we had to help them upon their feet. Lieutenant Bushong's horse was unable to stand, and we were compelled to leave him, expecting he would be devoured by wolves, but when we returned to camp we found him there. We buried our comrades with our butcher knives, placing their bodies in a deep buffalo trail, and carrying earth in our blankets to cover them from the nearest bluff, where it was readily scooped out. After we had thus covered their bodies as well as we could with earth, we laid heavy stones on top of all to prevent wolves from scratching them up. This was in July, 1861. We moved a short distance that day, and the next day our spies on the right flank reported they had seen Indians chasing buffalo. We started out for them at once, but only succeeded in running our horses down. Thinking the Indians would follow us, I left two men on good horses on our trail three miles from where we intended to camp, to keep watch, instructing them to remain there until dark. After night they came in and reported that the Indians were following us. That night I divided my whole force into fives, and placed them in squads around our horses, with orders that no one was to speak above a whisper.

Twice during the night the Indians attempted to get the horses, but failed both times. Some shots were fired at us. but none of us were hurt. It was a dark night, though clear, and the bushes and vines hanging over from the banks. of the ravine where we were encamped, made it still darker. Some of the men were encamped below and some above in the ravine. I inquired if there was any one who was willing to go into the dark hole or canon near by to ascertain if there were any Indians secreted there, Aaron Burr Brown, an eighteen year old boy, said: "Captain, suppose you go yourself, as you are getting the biggest pay for hunting Indians, and here is a good chance to find one if it is dark." I replied, "you go in with me," and in we went. We felt along the side of the bank where there was a hole in which we thought Indians might have secreted themselves, but did not discover any, although we found a horse. The next day we continued our route up the Brazos. We found fresh signs of Indians, and I am satisfied they would have attacked us had it not been that they discovered Major Burleson's command on the opposite side of the river.

Two of our men who had been wounded and lost during our chase after the Indians, supposed, it appears, that the rest of us had been killed. They made their way to Camp Cooper and reported that they were the only survivors of the fight. It was a long time before the report was corrected, as we were forty days in getting back to camp. I kept one scouting party out during the balance of that year. No conflicts with the Indians of any importance occurred until the winter set in. The Indians were depredating all the time on the settlements, but the settlers found it a very difficult matter to catch them, as well as we. They almost invariably managed to elude pursuit.

During the winter Captain Milton Boggess, with near half his company, and I with about half of mine, were going up Pecos river, and when near its head waters, we discovered an Indian camp in the distance, but their keen eyes had seen us first, and the Indians ran off, leaving their camp equipage, robes, blankets, etc., and some of their ponies and a large quantity of meat. We stopped in their camp and took possession of all we wanted. The next day we hunted them until night, but with no success. The day following, we discovered them a great distance off. I ordered the men to throw away every pound of extra weight, even including their ropes and hopples, and to run the Indians as long as one was to be seen. I told them if any one should fail to keep up with the rest, he would have to show bloody spurs as evidence that he tried to do so.

After running the Indians about eight miles, they began to leave their worst horses and double up on the best ones. John Hammock, of Gatesville, who was riding one of the best horses in my company, was ahead and fired the first shot at the Indians. The Indians then raised a white flag: but Hammock hallooed to them and told them that he had ridden too far to be swindled out of a fight in that sort of a style. The fight then began and soon grew pretty warm. Many of our horses had broken down in the chase, and it left us rather short of men, but our close, well directed shots soon told with fearful effect on the enemy, and they began to retreat. A running fight was kept up for several miles on the open plains, where not a bush or shrub was to be seen. The Indians were nearly all killed. Our men were well nigh worn out with fatigue, and two of them, Hardigree and Weston, were badly wounded.

I saw two of the Indians make off by themselves, and thought it strange. Sam Stills and I followed them. Our weapons were empty, and by the time we had loaded them we discovered that the two Indians were making for the head of the canon. I fired at one of them just as he went over the bluff into the head of the canon. Stills ran about one hundred and fifty yards below for the purpose of hiding himself in the brush at the bottom and killing the other Indian as he passed. He succeeded in doing so, but the one I shot at could not be found.

After the men who had fallen behind in the chase came up we made a thorough search for the Indian I had shot at, and found that he had been wounded and had secreted himself among the loose rocks that had fallen off the bluff.

While we were sitting on the rocks resting ourselves, Aaron Burr Brown said to me that if I would have him decently buried, and rocks put over him to prevent the wolves from scratching him up, in the event that he was killed, that he would go down among the rocks and try to finish the Indian I had wounded. I promised to do so, and off he went. Soon after disappearing from sight we heard him fire, and in a few moments we saw him coming out backwards from a crevice, the report of the pistol among the rocks having nearly stunned him. He waited until the smoke had cleared away, went in again and dragged out the dead body of the Indian.

On returning to where we had left our pack mules, we came across a fine-looking young Indian who had been slightly wounded in the hips. His comrades thinking, we suppose, that he was mortally hurt, had taken all his weapons from him except his butcher knife, but he fought desperately with that. The men scalped him before killing him, because the Indians had scalped Mr. Jackson alive a short time previously. The Indian complained greatly of the manner in which he was treated.

In April, 1862, we were ordered to Fort Mason for the purpose of being mustered out of the service. A party of Indians came in from the settlements with their booty, up the San Saba river, and passed near where we were encamped, Captain Boggess's company and my own. We immediately went in pursuit, and after a chase of ten or twelve miles we came up with them. They had abandoned all the horses they had stolen except those they were riding. As usual, they made fight, and gave us as much as we wanted to do until the men who had fallen behind in the chase came up.

One of the warriors had on a silk dress that had belonged to a lady who resided below on the San Saba. They had killed the whole family, and this scoundrel was wearing the dress of one of their murdered victims. The silk dress rattled as if it had adorned some city belle. Captain Boggess, thinking he was a squaw, called my attention to her, and asked me to notice "how viciously the damned squaw shot her arrows." He soon found out that a warrior's strength was inside that silken dress.

Some of the Indians were killed on the spot where the fight commenced, and the rest ran into a shin oak thicket, from which they fired on us with effect, killing or wounding horses and men at nearly every shot. Sergeant Erhenback was seriously wounded in several places. Mr. Johnston was also wounded, and Lieutenant Nelm's lips were pinned together with an arrow. Three or four of our horses were killed or wounded, one of which was my own. He was shot in the neck and shoulders with arrows. Three Indians were killed and another afterward died of his wounds.

Being now transferred to the Confederate service, I was placed in command of the regiment to fill the vacancy occasioned by the death of Col. Openchain, who had been killed. Colonel Malone was first ordered to take six companies and proceed to Columbus, and I soon afterward was ordered to march with the remaining four companies to Houston, thereby leaving the whole frontier west of the Brazos exposed, with no protection from the raids of the savages save what little the cow hunters could give.

Between six hundred and one thousand Indians soon after this made their appearance at or near Fort Murray, where about thirty families were forted up, inside of pickets driven in the ground, about eight miles from Fort Belknap. Several parties of these Indians raided the settlements below on the Brazos and murdered some families.

The first conflict they had was with Judge Harmison and his son Perry. They fought some sixty Indians for an hour. They retreated into a small mott of brushy timber and being armed with breech loading guns, they fired with such effect that they kept the Indians at bay until they heard the report of guns in another direction, and went off to ascertain the cause. The firing was by another party of Indians who had attacked and killed a man named Myers. When Myers was found afterward, it was evident from the signs that he had defended himself to the last against the fearful odds he had to contend with. He had undoubtedly caused several of the Indians to bite the dust. They butchered him in their usual savage manner, cutting out his heart and cutting off his hands which had hurled such destruction in their midst a few moments before.

The Indians then attacked the houses of Jodine Sprague, Carter, Hamby, and Joe Laker, killing some and capturing others. Susan Durken was left dead in the yard, she having refused to go with them as a prisoner they had killed her. They captured old Brit Johnson, a slave, who was attending to a ranch for Moses Johnson, near the mouth of Elm creek on the Brazos, in Young county. His family were all killed, excepting his wife and two of his children, who were carried into captivity.

After Brit was freed he spent more than three years among the Comanches before he succeeded in recovering his wife and children. The narrative of Brit's exploits, and how he finally succeeded in recovering his family, would be quite interesting had we space to go into details.

Doctor Wilson's wife and children and Mr. Hamby's wife and children, seeing the Indians across the Brazos, became alarmed, and when they heard of the murdering of their neighbors they tried to make their way to Bragg's ranch, known as Bragg's fort. As there was no chance to make fight against three hundred Indians, Wilson and Hamby concealed their families in a cave, hoping by showing themselves and making a feint of fighting by firing at them occasionally, to lead them away from the spot where they had hidden the women and children. In this they would probably have succeeded had it not been for some dogs that were with their families, whose barking led the Indians to where they were secreted. The Indians, not knowing who or how many were hid there, did not venture up, but called out in English to the women and children, telling them they were friends to the whites, etc. But the news they had heard of the previous massacres, and the arrows still sticking in several of the dogs that had run to them for their protection, gave the lie to all such assertions.

About this time some of the Indians attacked the house of Mr. George Bragg, to which Wilson and Hamby had fled after hiding their families, as previously stated. There were twenty-seven women and children and but five men in the house, to wit, George Bragg, Doctor Wilson, Mr. Hamby and his son, who was about grown, and a negro boy about eighteen years old. The rest of the men were off on a cow hunt, so there were but these five men to protect this house filled with women and children against hundreds of Indians. The women and children were directed to lie down upon the floor, so that the bullets and arrows might pass harmlessly over them. George Bragg had just built a small picket house without any shelter to the doors and windows. Many of the bullets and arrows shot by the Indians came through these open doors and windows, and Doctor Wilson was soon killed and Bragg fell mortally wounded, leaving only three to contend against such fearful odds. The Indians made a furious charge on the house before these men fell, but the men had plenty of guns and pistols well loaded, and they were used in such a manner as to kill and wound a number of the assailants. The Indians, however, succeeded in wounding Hamby several times, though not severely, and would have killed or carried into captivity the three remaining men, together with the women and children, but just then another party of about three hundred Indians had attacked Lieutenant Whitesides, of the border regiment, commanded by Colonel James Bourland, who had only forty-seven men and some citizens with him. Those attacking the, house hearing the firing, and not knowing the cause, fled in hot haste, leaving their dead and the battle ground in possession of the twenty-seven women and children, the wounded Mr. Hamby, his son and the negro boy.

The fight lasted about an hour. If ever men were heroes and deserved the thanks of their countrymen, assuredly the few who fought so nobly on that day, defending these helpless women and children, should not be forgotten.

The lieutenant, before mentioned, had succeeded in making his escape from the horde of savages that had surrounded him, and he and his party, together with some cow hunters, crossed the Brazos near Fort Murray.

The inmates of Fort Murray estimated the number of the Indians at from six hundred to a thousand. They were around the fort all day, and from their maneuvers it was supposed they intended to attack it. There were about eighty men in the fort, and perhaps about one hundred women and children.

The next day these Indians drove off a large number of cattle, estimated at from five to ten thousand head. A party followed them far enough to satisfy themselves that the cattle were being driven to Kansas for the use of the Federal army.

This formidable raid of the Indians caused a general. desertion of the organized northwestern frontier counties. The counties of Stephens, Palo Pinto, Jack, Wise and Montague were almost entirely abandoned by the settlers, only a few cowboys remaining at the large ranches—or, as they were then called, "forts." Not a living soul was left in Clay county. The last scout I made through that section, the houses and yards were as silent as the grave, all being deserted. The thirty-five thousand head of cattle on which this county had paid taxes to the government were all gone – gone to feed our enemies and to strengthen them for further destruction of our lives and property.

But I must not pass unnoticed the narrow escape made by my friend Bill Wooten from the Indians. He was living near Fort Belknap, and went off on a scout with a party of rangers- the same forty-five of the border regiment that fought against the six hundred Indians. The rangers were fighting against an overwhelming force, but when they saw that the Indians had completely surrounded the women and children, they did not stop to calculate the consequences, and rushed right in among them. Wooten having discharged all his shots, and, as it was no place to reload, started to run across a prairie about four miles wide, on foot, his horse having been killed under him. About forty Indians pursued him; but, as they perceived that two of the foremost Indians were pressing him closely, the rest turned back to follow the retreating rangers. After he had crossed the divide one of the Indians overtook him, drew his bow on him and said: "Run, Wooten, run, or I kill you. I know you. Do you know me? Long time ago you drive beef at Cooper; now Comanche drive beef heap."

Wooten made no reply, and the Indian did not attempt to shoot him. He reached home safely, but his clothes were nearly all gone, having been torn off by bushes and briars in his race for life. His run for life however left him an incurable invalid.

Another incursion was made by the Indians in the winter of 1863, while I was at Fort Belknap in command of six companies. Captain Guilentine, of the frontier militia, reported that the Kickapoos were in full force, and were passing up the Clear fork of the Brazos, near Phantom Hill,

At that time the Confederate authorities were pressed for soldiers and there was no force to spare for frontier service, but my command. The State of Texas exempted the frontier counties from conscription and organized all the citizens able to bear arms, for their defense, who scouted in companies by turns, the whole being placed under the command of Brigadier General James W. Throckmorton.

Captain Guilentine sent an express to the nearest militia captains at once. I despatched one hundred and ten Confederates under Captain Henry Fossett from the nearest Fort.

Captain Totten, of Bosque county, being the senior captain of militia, hurried to the objective point with what men he could collect, numbering over three hundred, making in all about four hundred and fifty men. This force pursued the Indians and followed their trail notwithstanding the ground was covered with snow, from a fearful snow storm. They crossed the Colorado and Concho rivers, and overtook the Indians at Dove creek. The Kickapoos, together with refugees from other tribes, numbered as estimated, about nine hundred. They took their position in a dense thicket, a deep ravine on one side and Dove creek on the other with its high bluffs. This left but few places open to attack.

Our officers held a consultation and the plan agreed upon was that Captain Totten, with the militia, should charge the thicket, and that Captain Fossett with his one hundred and ten men was to approach on horseback, take possession of the Indians' horses, if possible, and avail himself of any other advantages that might present themselves. Captain Fossett and his men captured all the Indian horses, with the exception of about fifty that were near the camp. They numbered between six hundred and one thousand head.

Captain Totten meeting with some delay in getting his. men across the deep ravine, got them somewhat out of order. Just then the Indians opened a heavy fire upon them from the thicket. The whites being in open prairie, across the ravine, were thrown into confusion. The most of the officers. with some of the men, having gained the thicket across the gulch, were nearly all killed or wounded. The Indians would have followed up their advantage with heavy slaughter to Captain Totten's men, but at that critical moment Captain Fossett, seeing the situation, left the herd of horses he had just captured and charged upon the thicket at the opposite side, right amongst the tents, wigwams, women and children, thus drawing the attention of the Indians and preventing them from following up the advantage they had gained over the militia. Their lodges extended along the bank of Dove creek for about a quarter of a mile, and Captain Fossett charged the whole length of the encampment, firing at whatever could be seen from the brush. The Indians, hearing the firing in the direction of their camp, hastened thither and came near cutting off all retreat from the thicket. Captain Fossett's men had discharged all their guns, and there was no time to reload. They were compelled to retreat, in many places in single file, and they suffered considerably. Among the killed of the Confederates was Lieutenant Giddeon, of Captain Rowland's company.

The Indians, having no other force to contend against, pursued them until they reached the open prairie, where another desperate struggle ensued around the horses, extending over several miles of ground. Captain Fossett, having to cover the retreat of the militia, was compelled to abandon a portion of the captured horses, but he succeeded in carrying off about three hundred head. When he came up to where Captain Totten had rallied the militia some ten or twelve miles from the scene of action, they halted there and laid on their arms until the next morning with the determination of renewing the fight next day, but a heavy snow storm set in during the night, which put an end to all further hostilities.

It continued snowing until the ground was covered three or four feet deep. Some of the men came very near freezing to death. Some of the horses, those that had been greatly fatigued in the fight, froze during the night.

Captain Totten returned to the battle ground and buried the dead. There were about fifty whites killed in this fight and probably about as many Indians. The Indians evidently thought themselves badly whipped, as they left their camp equipage and dead on the battle field. They fled across the Rio Grande into Mexico.

Among the last visits the Indians made to this (Bosque) county they stole many horses, and they also raided at the same time several of the adjoining counties. A good many small parties of citizens scoured the mountains in pursuit of the Indians, one of which, my neighbor, Bill Erwin, commanded, having with him his sons and stock hands, together with my sons and stockmen. He stopped one night near the Leon bottom. He put out two of the youngest boys, Will Barry and Jim Erwin to guard the horses, thinking there would be but little danger while cooking and eating supper, but the boys discovered some Indians reconnoitering the camp. They reported the fact to Captain Erwin, who took the older men and placed them in ambush near the horses. He then made the young men build up big fires and dance, sing and wrestle around them for about an hour and a half to make the Indians believe they had not been discovered. They all then laid down around the fires as if they were going to sleep. The ruse had the desired effect. The temptation to steal horses was too strong. About two hours afterwards the Indians crawled up noiselessly and approached the horses. When very near Captain Erwin and his men fired upon them and killed one of the Indians. They think they killed another but supposed he was carried off by his comrades.

Another party of Indians went out through the mountains and crossed the Paluxy into Hood county. When on the divide between the Paluxy and Brazos they were discovered by a party of whites from Hood and Erath counties. They pursued the Indians, who, after quite a race, took position in a thicket on a small branch. The creek had a hole of water in it about waist deep. The brush and vines hanging over this hole of water from the banks hid the Indians from view, and the whites were compelled to approach within a few yards of them before they could be seen. This gave them a great advantage over the whites. But, after some maneuvering, the whites obtained a favorable position and picked off the Indians one by one, until there was none left to inform Brother Tatum, of the Sill agency, of the massacre.

It finally reached his ears, however, through some cow hunters who were driving beeves to the agency to feed the squaws and pappooses while the warriors were plundering and murdering the settlers. Brother Tatum told the cow men that it was an outrageous act to have killed such an innocent party of Indians; that they were merely a doctor and his escort who were going into the settlements to get. roots and herbs for sick Indians, which grew there in greater abundance than anywhere else. This may have been so, but the settlers did not understand what benefit. the sick Indians would derive from their stolen horses. There were seven Indians in the doctor's party, and all of them were killed. Two of the whites were killed and several wounded.

About the same time this fight took place, twenty Indians were discovered on the Paluxy. Fifteen citizens, under Haley and McDowell, pursued them. They overtook the Indians, and a sharp skirmish ensued, which lasted some time, and resulted in the recapture of all the horses they had stolen. Several of the whites were wounded, but none killed. Several Indians were also wounded, but none killed, as far as known. The Indians fled in haste to some place of safety. This was near Hanna's mill, in Hood county.

[Note.—It is but proper to say that the Kickapoo Indians, who were attacked on Dove creek, afterward claimed that they were on their way to Mexico with their families, and that the attack made upon them was unjust and uncalled for.]

Chapter 20

Josiah Wilbarger

IN the spring of 1830, Stephen F. Austin came to his new colony, located on the upper Colorado, with two surveyors and the advance guard of emigrants for the purpose of establishing the surveys of those who had made their selections. Josiah Wilbarger and Reuben Hornsby were among those who had previously been over the ground and picked out locations for their headright leagues. Wilbarger had come to Texas from the State of Missouri as early as 1828 and first settled in Matagorda county, where he remained about one year and then moved up the Colorado. It was in about the month of March, 1830, that he selected for his headright survey a beautiful tract of land situated at the mouth of what is now known as Wilbarger creek, about ten miles above where the San Antonio and Nacogdoches road crosses the river where the town of Bastrop now is. After making his selection he immediately moved on his headright league with his family and two or three transient young men and built his occupation house, his nearest neighbor being about seventy-five miles down the river. In the month of April, Austin, with his surveying party, accompanied by Reuben Hornsby, Webber, Duty and others, who had also previously made their selections, arrived, and commenced work on the Colorado at the crossing of the San Antonio and Nacogdoches road. The river was meandered to the upper corner of the Jesse Tannehill league, when the party stopped work in the month of May. Wilbarger was the first and outside settler in Austin's new colony until July, 1832, when Reuben Hornsby came up from Bastrop (where he had stopped for a year or two) and occupied his league on the east bank of the Colorado river, some nine miles below the site of Austin.

Hornsby's house was always noted for hospitality, and he, like his neighbor Wilbarger, was remarkable for those virtues and that personal courage which made them both marked men among the early settlers. Young men who from time to time came up to the frontier to look at the country made Hornsby's house a stopping place, and were always gladly welcomed, for it was chiefly through such visits that news from the States was obtained. A more beautiful tract of land, even now, can nowhere be found than the league of land granted to Reuben Hornsby. Washed on the west by the Colorado, it stretches over a level valley about three miles wide to the east, and was, at the time of which we write, covered with wild rye, and looking like one vast green wheat field. Such was the valley in its virgin state which tempted Hornsby to build and risk his family outside of the settlements. Until a few years ago not an acre of that league of land had ever been sold, but it was all occupied by the children and grand children of the old pioneer, who lived out his four score years and died without a blemish on his character.

In the month of August, 1833, a man named Christian and his wife were living with Hornsby. Several young unmarried men were also stopping there. This was customary in those days, and the settlers were glad to have them for protection.

Two young men, Standifer and Haynie, had just come to the settlement from Missouri to look at the country. Early in August, Josiah Wilbarger came up to Hornsby's, and in company with Christian, Strother, Standifer and Haynie, rode out in a northwest direction to look at the country. When riding up Walnut creek, some five or six miles northwest of where the city of Austin stands, they discovered an Indian. He was hailed, but refused to parley with them, and made off in the direction of the mountains covered with cedar to the west of them. They gave chase and pursued him until he escaped to cover in the mountains near the head of Walnut creek, about where James Rogers afterwards settled.

Returning from the chase, they stopped to noon and refresh themselves, about one-half a mile up the branch above Pecan spring, and four miles east of where Austin afterwards was established, in sight of the road now leading from Austin to Manor. Wilbarger, Christian and Strother unsaddled and hoppled their horses, but Haynie and Standifer left their horses saddled and staked them to graze. While the men were eating they were suddenly fired on by Indians. The trees near them were not large and offered poor cover. Each man sprang to a tree and promptly returned the fire of the savages, who had stolen up afoot under cover of the brush and timber, having left their horses out of sight. Wilbarger's party had fired a couple of rounds when a ball struck Christian, breaking his thigh bone. Strother had already been mortally wounded. Wilbarger sprang to the side of Christian and set him up against his tree. Christian's gun was loaded but not primed. A ball from an Indian had bursted Christian's powder horn. Wilbarger primed his gun and then jumped again behind his own tree. At this time Wilbarger had an arrow through the calf of his leg and had received a flesh wound in the hip. Scarcely had

Figure 20.1: Scalping of Josiah Wilbarger.

Wilbarger regained the cover of the small tree, from which he fought, until his other leg was pierced with an arrow. Until this time Haynie and Standifer had helped sustain the fight, but when they saw Strother mortally wounded and Christian disabled, they made for their horses, which were yet saddled, and mounted them. Wilbarger finding himself deserted, hailed the fugitives and asked to be permitted to mount behind one of them if they would not stop and help fight. He ran to overtake them, wounded, as he was, for some little distance, when he was struck from behind by a ball which penetrated about the center of his neck and came out on the left side of his chin. He fell apparently dead, but though unable to move or speak, did not lose consciousness. He knew when the Indians came around him — when they stripped him naked and tore the scalp from his head. He says that though paralyzed and unable to move, he knew what was being done, and that when his scalp was torn from his skull it created no pain from which he could flinch, but sounded like distant thunder. The Indians cut the throats of Strother and Christian, but the character of Wilbarger's wound, no doubt, made them believe his neck was broken, and that he was surely dead. This saved his life.

When Wilbarger recovered consciousness the evening was far advanced. He had lost much blood, and the blood was still slowly ebbing from his wounds. He was alone in the wilderness, desperately wounded, naked and still bleeding. Consumed by an intolerable thirst, he dragged himself to a pool of water and lay down in it for an hour, when he became so chilled and numb that with difficulty he crawled out to dry land. Being warmed by the sun and exhausted by loss of blood, he fell into a profound sleep. When awakened, the blood had ceased to flow from the wound in his neck, but he was again consumed with thirst and hunger.

After going back to the pool and drinking, he crawled over the grass and devoured such snails as he could find, which appeased his hunger. The green flies had blown his wounds while he slept, and the maggots were at work, which pained and gave him fresh alarm. As night approached he determined to go as far as he could toward Reuben Hornsby's, about six miles distant. He had gone about six hundred yards when he sank to the ground exhausted, under a large post oak tree, and well nigh despairing of life. Those who have ever spent a summer in Austin know that in that climate the nights in summer are always cool, and before daybreak some covering is needed for comfort. Wilbarger, naked, wounded and feeble, suffered after midnight intensely from cold. No sound fell on his ear but the hooting of owls and the bark of the cayote wolf, while above him the bright silent stars seemed to mock his agony. We are now about to relate two incidents so mysterious that they would excite our incredulity were it not for the high character of those who to their dying day vouched for their truth.

As Wilbarger lay under the old oak tree, prone on the ground he distinctly saw, standing near him, the spirit of his sister Margaret Clifton, who had died the day before in Florisant, St. Louis county, Missouri. She said to him: "Brother Josiah, you are too weak to go by yourself. Remain here, and friends will come to take care of you before the setting of the sun." When she had said this she moved away in the direction of Hornsby's house. In vain he besought her to remain with him until help would come.

Haynie and Standifer, on reaching Hornsby's, had reported the death of their three companions, stating that they saw Wilbarger fall and about fifty Indians around him, and knew that he was dead. That night Mrs. Hornsby started from her sleep and waked her husband. She told him confidently that Wilbarger was alive; that she had seen him vividly in a dream, naked, scalped and wounded, but that she knew he lived. Soon she fell asleep and again Wilbarger appeared to her alive, but wounded, naked and scalped, so vividly that she again woke Mr. Hornsby and told him of her dream, saying: "I know that Wilbarger is not dead." So confident was she that she would not permit the men to sleep longer, but had their coffee and breakfast ready by day break and urged the men at the house to start to Wilbarger's relief.

The relief party consisted of Joseph Rogers, Reuben Hornsby, Webber, John Walters and others. As they approached the tree under which Wilbarger had passed the night, Rogers, who was in advance, saw Wilbarger, who was sitting at the root of a tree. He presented a ghastly sight, for his body was almost red with blood. Rogers, mistaking him for an Indian, said: "Here they are, boys." Then Wilbarger rose up and spoke, saying: "Don't shoot, it is Wilbarger." When the relief party started Mrs. Hornsby gave her husband three sheets, two of them were left over the bodies of Christian and Strother until the next day, when the men returned and buried them, and one was wrapped around Wilbarger, who was placed on Roger's horse. Hornsby being lighter than the rest mounted behind Wilbarger, and with his arms around him, sustained him in the saddle. The next day Wm. Hornsby (who is still living), Joseph Rogers, Walters and one or two others returned and buried Christian and Strother.

When Wilbarger was found the only particle of his clothing left by the savages was one sock. He had torn that from his foot, which was much swollen from an arrow wound in his leg, and had placed it on his naked skull from which the scalp had been taken. He was tenderly nursed at Hornby's for some days. His scalp wound was dressed with bear's oil, and when recovered sufficiently to move, he was placed in a sled, made by Billy Hornsby and Leman Barker (the father-in-law of Wilbarger) because he could not endure the motion of a wagon, and was thus conveyed several miles down the river to his own cabin. Josiah Wilbarger recovered and lived for eleven years. The scalp never grew entirely over the bone. A small spot in the middle of the wound remained bare, over which he always wore a covering. The bone became diseased and exfoliated, finally exposing the brain. His death was hastened, as Doctor Anderson, his physician, thought, by accidentally striking his head against the upper portion of a low door frame of his gin house many years after he was scalped. We have stated the facts as received from the lips of Josiah Wilbarger, who was the brother of the author of this book, and confirmed by Wm. Hornsby, who still lives, and others who are now dead.

The vision which so impressed Mrs. Hornsby was spoken of far and wide through the colony fifty years ago; for her earnest manner and perfect confidence that Wilbarger was alive, made, in connection with her vision and its realization, a profound impression on the men present, who spoke of it everywhere. There were no telegraphs in those days, and no means of knowing that Margaret, the sister, had died seven hundred miles away only the day before her brother was wounded. The story of her apparition, related before he knew that she was dead — her going in the direction of Hornsby's, and Mrs. Hornsby's strange vision, recurring after slumber, present a mystery that made then a deep impression and created a feeling of awe which, after the lapse of half a century, it still inspires. No man who knew them ever questioned the veracity of either Wilbarger or the Hornsbys, and Mrs. Hornsby was loved and reverenced by all who knew her.

We leave to those more learned the task of explaining the strange coincidence of the visions of Wilbarger and Mrs. Hornsby. It must remain a marvel and a mystery. Such things are not accidents; they tell us of a spirit world and of a God who "moves in a mysterious way his wonders to perform."

Josiah Wilbarger left a wife and five children. His widow, who afterwards married Talbert Chambers, was the second time left a widow, and resided, in 1888, in Bastrop county, about thirty-five miles below the city of Austin.

The eldest son, John, was killed many years after the death of his father by the Indians in west Texas, as related elsewhere in this book. Harvey, another son of Josiah, lived to raise a large family, when he died. His widow and only son live in Bastrop county. One married daughter lives at Georgetown and another at Belton, Texas. Of the brothers and sisters of Josiah Wilbarger who came to Texas in 1837, the author, and Sallie Wilbarger (who resides in Georgetown), are the only survivors. Matthias Wilbarger, a brother, and a sister, Mrs. W. C. Dalrymple, died many years ago. Mrs. Lewis Jones, another sister, died on the way to Texas.

So far as our knowledge extends, this was the first blood shed in Travis county at the hands of the implacable savages. It was but the beginning, however, of a bloody era which was soon to dawn upon the people of the Colorado.

Owing to the sparsely settled condition of the country, the Indians could slip in, commit murders, then slip out and return to their mountain homes with impunity. However, when the rich valleys of the Colorado became known, immigrants began to flock into Austin's new colony, and it was not long until the settlers grew sufficiently strong to organize for protection into minute companies which were placed under the command of Colonel Edward Burleson. These companies afforded great protection to the families, and no doubt saved many women and children from being murdered or carried off into a captivity worse than death. The settlers over on the Brazos, the

Guadalupe and Lavaca had likewise formed similar organizations, but notwithstanding the vigilance and untiring efforts of these companies in trying to protect the advance guard of civilization from the tomahawk and scalping knife of the hostile savages, the bloody traces of these demons could be seen here today. several miles distant tomorrow; and before they could be overtaken they would be far into the cedar brakes of the mountains, where they could not well be pursued.

Such was the unsettled condition of affairs in Travis county even as late as 1846, when with annexation came peace and happiness to a people who had been harassed upon one hand by the Mexican government and warlike tribes on the other, until their means had well nigh been spent and their patience exhausted.

Today we enjoy the blessings of prosperity, purchased with the blood and heroism of a sturdy class of pioneers whom any nation would delight to honor. There are but few of them left, but they stand like the giant oaks of the forest, storm beaten but living evidences of the distant past.

[Note. — The tree under which Wilbarger was sitting when found by the relief party stood just at the foot of the hill, on the east side of Pecan spring branch, about one hundred and fifty yards above where Pecan spring school house now stands, and about where the road leading from Austin to Manor leads up the hill beyond the crossing on the branch. Reuben Hornsby and his wife, Mrs. Sarah Hornsby, were the grand parents of M. M. Hornsby, whose term of office as sheriff of Travis county expired in 1888. When Mrs. Sarah Hibbins's son was captured from the Indians in 1836, near Austin, the barrel of the gun which Wilbarger had when he was scalped was also recovered. The stock had been broken.]

INDEX